The Outcome of Classical German Philosophy

Friedrich Engels on G. W. F. Hegel and Ludwig Feuerbach

By

Thomas Riggins

The Outcome of Classical German Philosophy Friedrich Engels on G. W. F. Hegel and Ludwig Feuerbach by Thomas Riggins

Ludwig Feuerbach and the End of Classical German Philosophy by Friedrich Engels (Nov. 28, 1820- Aug. 5, 1895)

Translated by the translation team at Progress Publishers, Moscow in 1946. First Published in 1886, in *Die Neue Zeit, Germany.*

© **Midwestern Marx Publishing Press**

The Publishing Press of

THE MIDWESTERN MARX INSTITUTE FOR MARXIST THEORY AND POLITICAL ANALYSIS

Formatting, copy editing, proofreading and cover design by Kyle Murdoch per direction of the publisher.

Summer, 2023

www.midwesternmarx.com

Dubuque, IA/Carbondale, IL USA

ISBN: 979-8-218-95982-1

Other Titles by
The Midwestern Marx Publishing Press

Reading the Classical Texts of Marxism (2022) by Thomas Riggins

Marxism and the Dialectical Materialist Worldview: An Anthology of Classical Marxist Texts on Dialectical Materialism (2022) by Carlos L. Garrido

Eurocommunism: A Critical Reading of Santiago Carrillo and Eurocommunist Revisionism 2022 by Thomas Riggins

No Great Wall: On the Continuities of the Chinese Revolution (2022) by Carlos Martinez

The Purity Fetish and the Crisis of Western Marxism (2023) by Carlos L. Garrido

Forthcoming Titles

Introduction to Dialectical Materialism The Marxist Worldview (1927–reprinting) by August Thalheimer (Classics of Marxism Series)

Education in the Age of Neoliberal Dystopia by Yanis Iqbal

Reproletarianization: The Death of the American Middle Class by Noah Khrachvik

What About Venezuela? How Socialism Worked in Venezuela and Why the US Needs It Too by Edward Liger Smith

Against the Fake Left: Marxist Critiques of Contemporary Radicalisms by various contributing authors including:

Gabriel Rockhill, John Bellamy Foster, William Robinson, Vivek Chibber, Salvador Rangel, Jennifer Ponce de León, Carlos Martinez, Carlos L. Garrido, Edward Smith, Noah Khrachvik, Thomas Riggins, and Hilbourne Watson

Christopher Caudwell and His Critics: A Study of Caudwell's Philosophy of Art and its Critical Responses by Thomas Riggins

Selected Works of Henry Winston by Carlos L. Garrido and Noah Khrachvik

Bertrand Russell: A Marxist Critique by Thomas Riggins

Imperialism and Its Misunderstandings by Radhika Desai and Alan Freeman

Hegel, Marxism, and Dialectics by Carlos L. Garrido

Anthology of Classical Writings on Imperialism and Anti-Imperialist Struggles by Alan Freeman and Radhika Desai

Table of Contents

Part One

Part One

The Outcome of Classical German Philosophy

by
Thomas Riggins

Introduction

In the middle of the 1880s Friedrich Engels was asked by the editors of *Die Neue Zeit*, the theoretical journal of the Social Democratic Party of Germany, to write a reply to the Danish philosopher C. N. Starcke's book, *Ludwig Feuerbach* (1885). This book was originally Starcke's (1858-1926) PhD dissertation in philosophy. In addition to *Ludwig Feuerbach,* Starcke also wrote *Baruch de Spinoza.* Interestingly, he was also interested, as was Engels, in the work of Lewis Henry Morgan (1818-1881) who published *Ancient Society* (*1877*). This work, as we know, inspired Engels to write *The Origin of the Family, Private Property and the State* (1884).

Starcke's book–*Die Primitive Familie in ihrer Entstehung und Entwickelung* (*The Origin and Development of the Primitive Family*) came out in 1888. He mentions Engels critically in passing. He was not a socialist but a left leaning liberal. He founded the Justice Party in Denmark in 1919, which still exists, on the principles of Henry George (1839-1897).

At any rate, it is Starcke's book on Feuerbach which set off some nostalgic memories within Engels. Memories that invoked feelings like those experienced when watching the film *The Way We Were,*[1] back to his and Marx's youth and the revolutionary era of forty years prior, back when the 1848 Revolution convulsed Europe. All that happened in Germany since then, Engels remarks, "has been merely a continuation of 1848, merely an execution of the testament of the revolution."

"Hegel" Chapter Analysis

1848 was the foster child of 1789. Both the French and German revolutions–1848 was pan European but greatly affected Germany–were preceded by new movements in philosophy–the Enlightenment in France, and Hegelianism in Germany.

Engels focuses on one sentence of Hegel (one of the most misunderstood of many), namely, the infamous, "All that is real is rational; and all that is rational is real."[2] The reactionaries of the world and the ultra-rights have loved this sentence, and have treated it as "a philosophical benediction bestowed upon despotism." In recent times prominent philosophers such as Bertrand Russell and Karl Popper took this as Hegel's meaning and denounced him as pro-fascist.

Engels, however, is going to defend Hegel and explain what he really means–this sentence needs to be seen in its proper context in Hegel's philosophy. "All that is real is rational; and all that is rational is real." "*Was vernünftig* [reasonable, rational] *ist, das ist wirklich* [real, actual] *und was wirklich ist, das ist vernünftig.*"

Engel points out a major qualification of this sentence and that is, in Hegel's words, "In the course of its development reality proves to be necessary." On the surface, this doesn't seem very helpful. The Trump administration was "actual," but was it "rational"? It was "real" but was it "necessary"? Well, it was necessary according to the US constitution and was actual and rational in that respect, but it lost its necessity in 2020 by that same constitution and became irrational and lost actuality. But was it necessary that Trump, not Mrs. Clinton, be president?

That depends on what you think the *Amerikanische Geist* (American Spirit) is.

What this means is that reality is in constant flux (you can't step into the same river twice as new waters are ever flowing) determined by the laws of dialectics. In human history, this means institutions which once were necessary for society to function and were considered rational become, with the further development of knowledge and science, irrational and non-functioning. Engels says nothing is real without qualification, its reality is contextual, and this context determines its rationality (reality) and a change of context can make it lose its rationality, its *raison d'être* and it eventually ceases to exist–it is no longer *vernünftig* (reasonable).

This is Hegel's view according to Engels: "All that is real in the sphere of human history becomes irrational in the course of time… everything that is rational in the minds of men is destined to become real, however much it may contradict existing apparent reality." This view constitutes the revolutionary essence of Hegel's philosophy. Truth, "the business of philosophy," is no longer a system of "dogmatic statements" (think of the creeds of various religions–*The Nicene Creed* or the *39 Articles of the Anglicans*).

Truth is relative to the historical development of human understanding and science "which ascends from lower to ever higher levels of knowledge without ever reaching" the end point of "absolute knowledge." Dialectical philosophy is the "reflection" of this process in the human brain. And we, dear reader, will understand both Hegel and Marxism-Leninism when this process is reflected in our own brain, and we no longer need prayer beads or unscientific religious dogmas to deal with reality (assuming this is not already the case).

3

Now, Engels says, this view he gives of Hegel's philosophy is the logical consequence of Hegel's ideas, but Hegel himself does not explicitly draw them. The dialectic is an endless project and the Absolute Idea, which harmonizes all reality, could never be reached, but Hegel, against his own dialectic, nevertheless reaches it, and it turns out to be Hegel's philosophy itself. Nevertheless, even though Hegel's system *per se* cannot be accepted, there was no field in philosophy, religion, history, ethics, or aesthetics that Hegel did not comprehend and make intellectual contributions to those of which still astound us (as they did in Engels's day).

Hegel's system ends up being used by both conservatives and radicals as the Absolute Idea seems to have so far become embodied in existing social striations of the more advanced developed parts of the world—or at least on the road to that end. But the dialectical method which negates whatever is to bring about new realities has no end point. In Hegel's day religion and politics were the most serious concerns of the educated classes and practical plans and programs were looked for in these two spheres of thought and action. "Whoever placed the emphasis on the Hegelian system could be fairly conservative in both spheres; whoever regarded the dialectical method as the main thing could belong to the most extreme opposition, both in religion and politics."

In the 1840s in Germany the conservative elements, for king, church, and country, justified their positions with the conservative tendencies in Hegel's thought, while the group of young radicals who were known as the "Young Hegelians" waged philosophical war on traditional religion and the Prussian state. Engels says the Hegelian "school" decomposed into several right and left factions arguing with each other.

4

Although Engels goes over the most important ideas of some of these 1840s thinkers, we will concentrate on the most important philosopher by far of the radical thinkers of this period, the one whose philosophy was transitional between Hegelianism and Marxism.

This is, of course, is the title character of the essay, Ludwig Feuerbach (1804-1872). In Feuerbach's *The Essence of Christianity* (1841) he wrote: "Nature exists independently of all philosophy." Here was the book that finally established materialism as the basic doctrine of any scientific outlook or philosophy. "Nothing exists outside nature and man, and the higher beings our religious fantasies have created are only the fantastic reflection of our own essence."

Although this was stated before Marx and Engels created what has become Dialectical materialism, and much of Feuerbach's philosophy has been sublated by later developments, at least these two views of Feuerbach's form the basis of Marxism-Leninism and the political and social praxis of all Communist Parties, not only in the United States, but throughout the world (except for those who have fallen into revisionism–á la Bernstein and/or have incorporated various mistaken ideas derived from opportunism and Eurocommunism into their programs and dogmatically adhere to them).

This book, Engels says, gave its readers a feeling of liberation from the old dogmas and the spell cast by idealism. He wrote, "How enthusiastically Marx greeted the new conception and how much–in spite of all critical reservations–he was influenced by it, one may read in *The Holy Family.[3]*"

Engels ends part one (of four) of his work by remarking that the Revolution of 1848 eclipsed all of these philosophical disputes and not only the Young Hegelian's, but both Hegel and Feuerbach themselves, were pushed aside in the ongoing political eruptions occasioned by the revolutionary activity of the masses.

"Materialism" Chapter Analysis

Engels opens the second part of his essay by saying: "The great basic question of all, especially of latter-day philosophy, is that concerning the relation of thinking and being." This is one of the oldest questions humans have been interested in, dating back to the earliest appearance of self-consciousness in our species. As we tried to understand the world around us and the forces of nature and the other animals we lived with and were surrounded by, we thought of them as somewhat like ourselves, with some awareness or spirit, and primitive religious views began to develop in our consciousness–such as the idea that there are nature spirits to be appeased, and finally powerful gods and goddesses that could help or hurt humans. We ended up thinking that the world was created by the gods, and finally a supreme God who was also responsible for the existence of humans. Until the creation of modern science, the question was: which came first, nature or the creators of nature, the spirits or God? The question was answered: thinking, the gods, and mind came first and then nature.

Philosophy, religion, and science began to consolidate around two great schools of thought with regard to this question:

1. Idealism; God and thinking first, man and nature second
2. Materialism; nature and man first, and only then can self-consciousness develop in humans, and

ultimately, can thinking create the notions of gods and God in its own image–the image of humans.

Engels was interested in the state of this argument in his day, when the great champion of idealism was Hegel and his system, and materialism was attacking this system in the form of Feuerbach's philosophy, but more importantly, in the new and improved form that grew out of a synthesis of Hegel's logical (metaphysical) methods and Feuerbach's materialism which became Marxism, and which is known today as Marxism-Leninism (AKA Dialectical materialism). Marxism-Leninism is the result of the development of Marxist theory by Lenin and the experiences of the Russian Revolution. It is based on the belief that the Lenin/Russian Revolution experience still has relevance today for the transition from capitalism to socialism.

Next, Engels points out, we have to ask what is the relation of our thinking to the world, to nature? Can we get a correct reflection of the external world in our ideas of it? The majority of philosophers say, yes. For Hegel thinking recognizes itself in the world. Our ideas are part of the development in time of the Absolute Idea which has existed before the world from eternity. This is similar to Plato's view of the things in the external world being imperfect reflections of the world of ideas which exist in "heaven" (or the Mind of God in the Christian view based on Plato). Hegel makes the mistake, as all systematic philosophers do, that since he thinks he has figured out the correct relation between thinking and being (being in the real world) his philosophy is the only correct one.

Besides materialism there have always been, and still are, practitioners of idealism. In his day David Hume in the United Kingdom and Immanuel Kant in Germany were the most well-known. Hume was a skeptic, thinking the mind could never get to the basic reality of things (objective or subjective) and Kant also had a similar idea but was not a skeptic. The mind could understand the way the world interacted with it but the things in the world were "for us," that is, filtered by our perceptions. Therefore, we could never know what they were "in themselves" unperceived. For Engels, Kant took care of Hume and Hegel took care of Kant. Feuerbach took care of Hegel and Marx perfected the materialism of Feuerbach. The problem was how to get proof for the idea that nature was real, outside of us, and understandable. This was not a philosophical solution, but a scientific one. The answer, according to Engels, was a practical one. We can postulate how nature works and then test our ideas. If we can predict what will happen and it comes about, that is evidence of its independent existence, since our theory doesn't compel nature to act a certain way, we must adapt our theory to how nature acts independently of us. This is for Engels the proof of materialism.

Engels now turns to a quote by Feuerbach cited in Starcke's text. Engels doesn't deal with much of the book (*The Origin and Development of the Primitive Family*) itself, nor do we have to, as he says, it is "loaded with a ballast of philosophical phraseology." Feuerbach has taken Hegel's logic, which is based on the view that the categories of logic are eternal and preexist the actual physical world (this entails a complicated metaphysical argument) and demonstrates that the logic is a product of our minds (which are animal minds) and a part of the physical world from which we developed (Darwin's theory which came later confirms this). This is materialism, says Engels, but Feuerbach himself hesitates to completely affirm it. Here is Feuerbach's quote cited by Starcke: "To me materialism is the foundation of the edifice of human essence and

9

knowledge; but to me it is not what it is to the scientists and necessarily is from their standpoint and profession, namely, the edifice itself. Backwards I fully agree with the materialists; but not forwards."

What's going on here? Engels says Feuerbach has mixed up the general concept of materialism (matter first, mind second) with the particular form this concept assumed in the 18th century–a crude mechanical materialism that existed before the development of the Hegelian dialectic and which was still being preached in the time of Feuerbach by the natural scientists and medical doctors who had not, for the most, part studied the logic of the Hegelian system. In the same way that 18th century idealism evolved and developed into Hegelianism, so materialism evolved and developed into a more sophisticated form as the result of the development of science in the 19th century. Feuerbach, I think, as a student of Hegel should have known this, but Engels holds that he never properly understood Hegel's dialectic.

There were two limitations that were responsible for the mechanical nature of 18th century materialism. The first was the state of science at that time, which was dominated by the mechanistic universe of the Newtonian system. This mechanistic worldview was applied not only to physics, but to biology and chemistry as well, when both of the latter two sciences were just in their infancy compared to physics, and higher laws of process and change played second fiddle to mechanics. This was also true in geology at that time when the age of the earth was still considered to be rather young due to Biblical influences.

The second limitation was related to the first–this was "the inability to comprehend the world as a process." This also applied to the concepts of history. Everywhere there were essential unchanging factors at work that were cyclical in nature. Civilizations started out small, grew, and collapsed, and the cycle then repeated itself. Even Hegel, Engels maintains, fell victim to this mechanical essentialism with his philosophical system, although it contradicted his philosophical method which was dialectical and not mechanical. It took the work of Feuerbach and later Marx (and Engels as well) to overcome this contradiction. Nature operates according to the laws of Hegel's logic, which are external to Nature, and Nature is an alienation of matter from its essential logical being. But the concepts of the logic start from primitive notions (Being versus Nothingness leading to Becoming, etc.,) until the whole of the system culminates due to permutations, contradictions, development of new concepts, etc., until the Absolute Idea is arrived at.

The logical world is one of process, evolution, change, and progressive development; but the world of man (history) and nature are just mechanical reflections of this system of logic. Matter is inert and non-dialectical. This is the conservative element in Hegel. His system was supposed to justify the world as it is, and the ruling classes of his day appreciated this. Engels says, "the method, for the sake of the system, had to become untrue to itself." But lurking within the Hegelian system was this revolutionary method, which was disinterred by Marx and Engels, a method which could lead to the overthrow of "what is" and its replacement with a revolutionary new world order. The history of the last two centuries has been the painful labor of the world process to deliver and bring to birth the resolution of this contradiction.

It was during this period, the mid-19th century, that history too began to be studied in a scientific manner. The bourgeois materialists descending from the 18th century didn't see history as a developing progressive process. The Middle Ages, for example, were dismissed as a backward era that had to be overcome to get civilization back on the track laid out in the classical era of Greece and Rome. Engels says this is all wrong–the Middle Ages were a time of great progress marked by the "extension" of European civilization, the consolidation of the nation state, and technical advances that the 14th and 15th centuries introduced. It wasn't until after the 1848 Revolutions that scientific history really got off the ground, stimulated by the rapid development of the natural sciences.

Engels now seeks to explain why Feuerbach's materialism, while it stood head and shoulders above the old mechanical materialism inherited from the Enlightenment, still missed the boat and did not really become modern enough to serve as the basis of the materialist worldview of Marx and Engels. It was not really the fault of Feuerbach. Because his philosophy was progressive and ahead of his time he was banished from Academia for political reasons and ended up living out in the boondocks cut off from the intellectual ferment going on in post 1848 Europe. Therefore, he was not able to fully update his materialism to the dialectical level that Marx and Engels achieved.

We will soon see, in, part three ("Feuerbach" Chapter Analysis) to what extent Feuerbach still had some views based on idealism, but first we must go over a critique of Starcke's views about Feuerbach's "idealism." Engels says Starcke found Feuerbach's "idealism" in "the wrong place." Here is what Starcke says: "Feuerbach is an idealist; he believes in the progress of mankind." As far as Feuerbach's philosophy is concerned, Starcke continues, "The foundation, the substructure of the whole, remains nevertheless idealism. Realism [Materialism-TR] is for us nothing more than a protection against aberrations, while we follow our ideal trends. Are not compassion, love, enthusiasm for truth and justice ideal forces?"

Starcke here confuses ethical commitments to "ideals" that people have with the philosophy of idealism, which maintains that the basis of existence, of Being, is ontologically some mental or spiritual essence or substance that predates matter and from which the material universe derives its being. These are two entirely different uses of the word "idealism," and we should not confuse them. If Starcke doesn't understand this difference, then "he has lost all meaning of these terms" in this context.

"Feuerbach" Chapter Analysis

So, what kind of idealism is Feuerbach, according to Engels, peddling? Feuerbach is a materialist who wants to advocate a true religion for humanity. Here is a quote from him: "The periods of humanity are distinguished only by religious changes. A historical movement is fundamental only when it is rooted in the hearts of men. The heart is not a form of religion, that the latter should exist also in the heart; the heart is the essence of religion." Religion is based on the love that humans are capable of sharing with one another. Heretofore that love has been objectified and projected upon mythical beings and has been the alienated essence of the historic religions as well as the natural religions of primitive times.

Now, in the modern world of scientific understanding, we can dispense with the mythical superstitious religious beliefs that dominate the masses (they will have to be educated of course) and have a loving religion of the heart directly practiced by humans, Engels says, "this becomes the love between 'I' and 'Thou.'" Sex is the highest way we can express our love; so, sexual relations become one of the highest forms of Feuerbach's new religion.

Sexual attraction and love making are purely natural functions of the human being and they should not be circumscribed by the rules and regulations of the state or of the positive religions (positive = historically existing). All the rules and regulations about sex and the relations between loving humans that are associated with, for example, Christianity, Islam, Judaism and Buddhism should be dumped as they are based on illusions and mythological premises. But the idealism that Feuerbach manifests comes from his view that these relations do need a religious foundation, not from the positive or primitive religions, but based on the "human heart." Speaking strictly as a materialist, the "heart" is a muscle, just as the ischiocavernosus muscle, so Feuerbach is being metaphorical. Anyway, Engels says, the major point is "not that these purely human relations exist, but that they shall be conceived of as the new, true religion."

Here Feuerbach is a victim of his era: religion is important, and Feuerbach wants to keep the word around–he thinks it is important to have a society based on "religion." Engels thinks it's really ridiculous to try and have a materialist religion, one without a "God" or any supernatural ideas attached to it. The idea that religious changes are what delimit the periods of humanity is, Engels says: "Decidedly false."

For Marxists, As Engels notes, the great epochal changes in history are economically based on changes in class relations and power politics; religious changes only accompanied these events. Meanwhile, there can be no "I-Thou" lovey-dovey relationships between humans as humans based on the natural proclivity for people to love one another, because our world and the globalized society we are all living in is still "based upon class antagonism and class rule." Feuerbach's writings on the religion of love, Engels points out, are "totally unreadable today."

Religion remains in the 21st century what it has always been–the opium of the masses. We can work with religious people on specific progressive projects, but we should not encourage religious belief because such beliefs are rooted in Idealistic unscientific notions which prevent people from a proper understanding of reality–and this holds back the movement towards human liberation and in the long run only helps the exploiters.

Despite his writings on religions, Feuerbach has only really studied one, according to Engels, i.e., Christianity. Not only that, but it is an abstract idealized form of Christian morality which Feuerbach thinks his new religion of the heart, based on sexual intercourse, will instill in humanity. What is this "humanity" that he writes about? It is an abstract and idealized humanity that Feuerbach finds existing in all ages and climes. It is an ahistorical concept–some kind of "human nature" that Feuerbach had deduced by his concept of Christian morality.

Engels contrasts the materialist Feuerbach with the objective idealist Hegel, who also writes about Christianity and morals. Despite outward appearances, the materialist is really an idealist and the idealist a materialist. Feuerbach is a materialist because he doesn't believe in God or a supernatural world on which to base his new religion; he bases it on the materially existing species of man on our planet and on nothing else. Sexual intercourse is at the heart of the new religion. It is really rooted in material existence. Yet his moral system is an abstract one deduced from an ideal Christianity.

Christianity, Jesus, God, etc., is nothing more than a human reflection projected into the sky for Feuerbach–the human family is the source of all the ideals about the Holy Family, morality is just this reflection coming back to us of our own dreams and ideals. But for Engels, this reflection is devoid of the actual behavior of Christians throughout history who, besides engaging in sexual intercourse, have done a lot of unsavory activities inspired by their religion. Feuerbach who "preaches sensuousness, immersion in the concrete, in actuality, becomes thoroughly abstract as soon as he begins to talk of any other than mere sexual intercourse between human

16

beings." So, the materialist has produced a philosophy based on abstract mental constructions he has deduced from the Christian religion which is the basis for his morality. This is why the materialist is an idealist! A living breathing unity of opposites (at least until 1872).

And what of Hegel? Was Feuerbach actually an improvement on Hegel? Well, here is Feuerbach's morality in a nutshell. All human beings have an innate desire for "bliss;" but we can't attain bliss without knowing how not to overindulge our desires, and we must also respect the social rights of others to also attain bliss–and this we do through love. Engels writes, "Rational self-restraint with regard to ourselves and love in contact with others–these are the basic rules of Feuerbach's morality; from them all others are derived."

Despite all Feuerbach's comments about materialism, these rules about morality are, Engels says, banal. You can't find "bliss" by just thinking about yourself and it is impossible to practice "love" towards others in the real world due to the actual social and economic systems humans live in. Feudal lords and surfs, slaves and masters, and in our age capitalists and proletarians are proof of the banality of Feuerbach's pretensions to morality. Ruling (and exploiting) and ruled (and exploited) classes existing under the same social totality means that the masses will always be deprived of the material needs they require–both to find a blissful life for themselves, or to properly be able to practice unselfish "love" for others, especially for those who oppress them.

In this respect, Hegel was more advanced than Feuerbach. Hegel saw morality as advancing through historical stages driven by humanity's "greed and lust for power." Hegel explained how in each stage this struggle produced contradictions that could be resolved only by moving on to a higher stage of moral

17

consciousness, until we reached Hegel's day, when the idea of human equality had reached its highest bourgeois level (with the French Revolution)–all men are equal before the law (the level including women was yet to come). There was an innate drive here also, the struggle for human freedom–which was an idea struggling to come to human consciousness and history–was the result of this struggle. This was Hegel's idealism.

For Marxists, it will be the class struggle objectively working in the material life of human beings at any point in history that is responsible for "moral" progress. "The cult of abstract man, which formed the kernel of Feuerbach's new religion, had to be replaced by the science of real men and their historical development. This further development of Feuerbach's standpoint beyond Feuerbach was inaugurated by Marx in 1845 in *The Holy Family*." [Although this work was a joint creation of Marx and Engels, Engels here credits Marx with the breakthrough beyond Feuerbach's materialism to what was to become Dialectical materialism.]

"Marx" Chapter Analysis

Engels begins this part by discussing the disintegration of
Hegelian philosophy that set in shortly after Hegel's death.
Two basic schools grew out of Hegel's thought–the Left
Hegelians and the Right Hegelians. The Right Hegelians went
down the road of conservative acceptance of the establishment
and became reactionary upholders of the status quo, we have
no need to discuss these philosophical losers.

The Left Hegelians became liberals and radical bourgeois
thinkers. They did some progressive work in theology writing
about religion as a subject to be studied outside of the supernatural framework of traditional belief. Only one of the Left
Hegelians left any imprint behind in the field of philosophy and
that was Feuerbach. We have seen above what Engels thought
of the limitations of his materialism and its contamination with
religious and moral arguments. Important as Feuerbach was, he
was a pipsqueak compared to Hegel, the depth of whose philosophy he failed to grasp. Engels sums up Feuerbach thusly:
"He could not cope with Hegel through criticism; he simply
cast him aside as useless, while he himself, compared to the
encyclopedic wealth of the Hegelian system, achieved nothing
positive beyond a bombastic religion of love and a meagre, impotent morality."

However, besides the Right and Left Hegelians there was a
third philosophical development that came into existence and
pointed out a viable philosophical future for a core set of beliefs that can benefit humanity and solve the social problems
facing it. Engels writes "this tendency is essentially connected

with the name of Marx." At this point Engels inserts an important footnote that not only explains his relations to Marx by way of the new idea of scientific socialism and why it richly deserves to be named after him as "Marxism."

This should calm down those so-called "Marxists" who wish to avoid using the term "Marxism" to opportunistically have a more public appeal. Here is an example from a would be "Scientific Socialist" concerning the use of the term "Marxism:"

> "'Marxism, Marxism-Leninism.' Very bad idea to name a scientific worldview after individuals. Way too subjective and besides too many bad stories and nightmares associated with it. And, not very working-class sounding. Too many syllables and hyphens. Replace it with 'scientific socialism' or the 'socialist and communist idea.'"[4]

We certainly don't want to overwhelm working people with syllables and hyphens!

But Engels notes that this great new theory about the nature of socialism which he and Marx elaborated, the theory that explains the working of capitalism and the way the exploitation of humans by humans can finally be ended, is totally world changing–up there with the ideas of Darwin and Newton (Einstein now). And yes, Engels, helped develop this new world outlook, but it was Marx who really worked out the details and developed the major ideas of the theory. Engels helped but Marx could have done it alone and Engels could not have. "Without him," Engels says, "the theory would not be by far what it is today. It thereby rightly bears his name."

How anyone that came to be a follower of this theory yet maintains that Marx's name, or his name conjoined with Lenin's, is associated with "too many bad stories and nightmares" is a puzzlement–as only the capitalists, imperialists and other enemies of humanity should be having nightmares when they hear about Marxism. The comrades should be celebrating it.

But, just what did Marx do? He really established materialism as the philosophy of the left after Hegel's philosophy became outmoded–a real materialism unlike the soft-core materialism of Feuerbach. Marx's materialism was dedicated to viewing the real world just as it presented itself to us free of idealistic prejudices. Engels and Marx "decided mercilessly to sacrifice every idealist quirk which could not be brought into harmony with the facts conceived in their own, and not in a fantastic, interconnection. And materialism means nothing more than this."

But Hegel was not really outmoded, at least not completely. His idealistic explanations for the changes observed in history and science were discarded but NOT his method of analysis–i.e., his dialectical method of seeing the world as a process of change, development, and contradiction, rather than one of unchanging essences which only seem to be involved in such changes which are really reduced to never changing first essences.

For Hegel it all begins with the idea of the CONCEPT– there is just a given absolute first concept which contains in itself from eternity all the laws and principles, which Hegel lays out in his Science of Logic. Engels says this Concept is the "soul of the universe." Hegel says it is "God as he is in his eternal essence before the creation of nature and a finite mind." The word "God" doesn't mean what it means in any of the world's great religions–it's a Hegel thing. This Concept is all worked out like the rules of chess, only before there is any real material chess board or pieces that must move by these rules. In nature they become revealed as they develop as a result of the resolution of contradictions they engender.

The Concept, God, somehow "alienates itself" by coming into existence as Nature–it is not at this point self-conscious. It is like that singularity that became the Big Bang which contained the seeds of all the laws of nature and math, etc. that exist in our universe. The Rules of Chess contain every possible move in every possible game now and for all future time–but the Rules of Chess are not self-conscious, and neither is the Concept/God/Nature (yet). It becomes self-conscious when humans become self-conscious. Engels continues, "This self-consciousness then elaborates itself again in history from the crude form until finally the absolute concept (God) comes to itself completely in Hegelian philosophy." History is the record of this trip and self-consciousness advances progressively through time to the modern world. This is an unfolding that human self-consciousness becomes aware of, but it is independent of human self-consciousness which is just the mirror which reflects it.

Well, Engels says, "This ideological perversion had to be done away with." Marxist materialism means we comprehend our mental concepts as "images of real things instead of regarding the real things as images of some or other stage of the absolute concept." The great basic thought of Hegel was that that reality is not a stable fixed collection of things to be studied but a PROCESS "in which the apparently stable things, no less than their mental images in our heads, the concepts, go through uninterrupted change of coming into being and passing away, in which, for all apparent accidentally and despite all temporary retrogression, a progressive development asserts itself in the end."

If this materialist dialectic, the correction of Hegel by Marx, is correct, we should see the dissolution of the Soviet Union as a "temporary retrogression" and the resulting Russian Federation as a "progressive development." OR we can see the dissolution of the Soviet Union and the birth of the Russian Federation and other post-soviet states as an ongoing retrogression that will eventually rebound in a progressive resolution. The predictive value of Marxist philosophy, however, does not have a sterling track record. This view, of a coming necessary progressive rebound, has religious overtones that Engels would not appreciate.

Why two terms "Dialectical Materialism" and "Historical Materialism"? It is because the dialectic is different when applied to nature than to history. Dialectical Materialism is the overall name of the philosophy and Historical Materialism is a subdivision. The dialectic at work in nature reveals that "nothing happens as a consciously desired aim." Sorry God, no divine plan just *natura naturata* (nature already created). "In the history of society, on the contrary, the actors are all endowed with consciousness... nothing happens without a desired aim."

Nevertheless, there are general laws of history at work, which is one of the reasons so many of our aims and plans either fail or backfire and "the best laid schemes of mice and men" *gang aft agley*" (often go wrong). History looks like just chance events or as "just one damn thing after another"[5] but, according to Engels, "wherever on the surface chance holds sway, it is always governed by inner hidden laws and these laws only have to be discovered." This is the Marxist version of Adam Smith's "the invisible hand" and Hegel's "the cunning of reason" (*die List der Vernunft*).

By the time Engels was writing this work, the mid-late 19th century, the class struggle, the major motivating force behind historical development, had reached the point that in the most developed countries where, what had been a three way class struggle in Europe since the end of the Middle Ages for production and control of the economy between the class possessing agricultural production (the nobility) the capitalists (the bourgeoisie) who controlled the instruments of production involved in capital formation by means of industry and commerce, and the working people who owned no significant property beyond their bodies and ability to employ them in the service of others (the proletariat, both industrial and agricultural) had now boiled down to essentially a struggle between two of those classes, the bourgeoisie and the proletariat; other classes and strata were insignificant and play only a supporting role to the two major contenders.

This struggle plays out in the political arena, but politics is only the reflection of economic interests–the economic struggle is the primary struggle. Control of the state is a political struggle. But, Engels says, "the state–the political order–is the subordinate factor and civil society–the realm of economic relations–the decisive element." Hegel had it the other way around, another difference between Marxism and Hegelianism. If we really study modern conditions "we discover that in modern history the will of the state is, on the whole, determined by the changing needs of civil society, by the supremacy of this or that class, in the last resort, by the development of the productive forces and relations of exchange."

The class struggle, in so far as it aims at realizing state power, takes the form of a political struggle. Politics involves ideological conflicts, and it often happens that the participants lose contact consciously with the true economic foundations that underlie this struggle. In the West the struggle between the bourgeoisie and the nobility took the form of political struggle in the guise of religion, Catholicism versus Protestantism–this took the consciousness of the economic issues even further away from people's awareness. Protestant Christianity was the vehicle by which the bourgeoisie ousted the feudal order from the control of the economic base of civil society.

Protestantism in its Calvinist form was especially triumphant. In the Enlightenment Catholicism was discredited and Protestantism opened the way to Freethinking, Deism and the rejection of Christianity by the intellectuals of the new bourgeois ruling class that came to power in the great French Revolution. Once in power, religion was domesticated and used by the new ruling class to control the masses. The pope today is just a sweet little old man who protects pedophiles and doesn't want women to control their own reproductive organs. Protestant preachers are basically shills collecting money from their congregants (with few exceptions).

Religion is useful in some civil rights contexts to motivate progressive actions from populations cut off from effective political paths to control their own lives, but Engels concludes that we are in the final stage of Christianity (this applies to religion in general). It has "become incapable of continuing to serve any progressive class as the ideological garb of its aspirations." At this point in history the proper garb for the proletariat and working people in general (which make up the only progressive class under capitalism) is some form of Marxism (or Marxism-Leninism particularly) and, unfortunately, the reactionary bourgeoisie is in control of all the major political forces in the world, in one way or another, outside of a few bastions of Marxism that survived the implosion of the Soviet Union and its allied states.

With no really progressive role left for religion, and the end of classical German philosophy, as well as philosophy *qua* (is so far as) philosophy being replaced by science, we have arrived at a situation, as Jean Paul Sartre admitted, where Marxism is the only philosophy that can be utilized to explain today's world and its possible progressive future. Engels concludes his book with the following: "The German working-class movement is the heir to German classical philosophy." Well, the German working class hasn't taken care of its inheritance, but it can still live up to Engels's expectations. Nowadays it's the world working class that is heir to classical German philosophy, as well as to classical Chinese philosophy (esp. Confucianism), and to the materialist-based philosophies of other cultural traditions (e.g., Charvaka, also known as Lokayatain, in India and forms of Buddhism not inconsistent with modern science).

Part Two

Ludwig Feuerbach and the Outcome of Classical German Philosophy

by
Friedrich Engels

Forward

In the preface to *A Contribution to the Critique of Political Economy*, published in Berlin, 1859, Karl Marx relates how the two of us in Brussels in the year 1845 set about: "to work out in common the opposition of our view"–the materialist conception of history which was elaborated mainly by Marx–to the ideological view of German philosophy, in fact, to settle accounts with our erstwhile philosophical conscience. The resolve was carried out in the form of a criticism of post-Hegelian philosophy. The manuscript, two large octavo volumes, had long reached its place of publication in Westphalia when we received the news that altered circumstances did not allow of its being printed. We abandoned the manuscript to the gnawing criticism of the mice all the more willingly as we had achieved our main purpose–self-clarification!

Since then more than 40 years have elapsed and Marx died without either of us having had an opportunity of returning to the subject. We have expressed ourselves in various places regarding our relation to Hegel, but nowhere in a comprehensive, connected account. To Feuerbach, who after all in many respects forms an intermediate link between Hegelian philosophy and our conception, we never returned.

In the meantime, the Marxist world outlook has found representatives far beyond the boundaries of Germany and Europe and in all the literary languages of the world. On the other hand, classical German philosophy is experiencing a kind of rebirth abroad, especially in England and Scandinavia, and even in Germany itself people appear to be getting tired of the pauper's broth of eclecticism which is ladled out in the universities there under the name of philosophy.

In these circumstances, a short, coherent account of our relation to the Hegelian philosophy, of how we proceeded, as well as of how we separated, from it, appeared to me to be required more and more. Equally, a full acknowledgement of the influence which Feuerbach, more than any other post-Hegelian philosopher, had upon us during our period of storm and stress, appeared to me to be an undischarged debt of honor. I therefore willingly seized the opportunity when the editors of *Neue Zeit* asked me for a critical review of Starcke's book on Feuerbach. My contribution was published in that journal in the fourth and fifth numbers of 1886 and appears here in revised form as a separate publication.

Before sending these lines to press, I have once again ferreted out and looked over the old manuscript of 1845–46 (*The German Ideology*).

The section dealing with Feuerbach is not completed. The finished portion consists of an exposition of the materialist conception of history which proves only how incomplete our knowledge of economic history still was at that time. It contains no criticism of Feuerbach's doctrine itself; for the present purposes, therefore, it was unusable. On the other hand, in an old notebook of Marx's I have found the *11 Theses on Feuerbach*, printed here as an appendix.

These are notes hurriedly scribbled down for later elaboration, absolutely not intended for publication, but invaluable as the first document in which is deposited the brilliant germ of the new world outlook.

Frederick Engels,
London,
February 21, 1888

Hegel

The volume before us carries us back to a period which, although in time no more than a generation behind us, has become as foreign to the present generation in Germany as if it were already a hundred years old. Yet it was the period of Germany's preparation for the Revolution of 1848; and all that has happened since then in our country has been merely a continuation of 1848, merely the execution of the last will and testament of the revolution.

Just as in France in the 18th century, so in Germany in the 19th, a philosophical revolution ushered in the political collapse. But how different the two looked! The French were in open combat against all official science, against the church and often also against the state; their writings were printed across the frontier, in Holland or England, while they themselves were often in jeopardy of imprisonment in the Bastille. On the other hand, the Germans were professors, state-appointed instructors of youth; their writings were recognized textbooks, and the termination system of the whole development–the Hegelian system–was even raised, as it were, to the rank of a royal Prussian philosophy of state! Was it possible that a revolution could hide behind these professors, behind their obscure, pedantic phrases, their ponderous, wearisome sentences? Were not precisely these people who were then regarded as the representatives of the revolution, the liberals, the bitterest opponents of this brain-confusing philosophy? But what neither the government nor the liberals saw was seen at least by one man as early as 1833, and this man was indeed none other than Heinrich Heine.

Let us take an example. No philosophical proposition has earned more gratitude from narrow-minded governments and wrath from equally narrow-minded liberals than Hegel's famous statement: "All that is real is rational; and all that is rational is real." That was tangibly a sanctification of things that be, a philosophical benediction bestowed upon despotism, police government, Star Chamber proceedings and censorship. That is how Frederick William III and how his subjects understood it. But according to Hegel certainly not everything that exists is also real, without further qualification. For Hegel the attribute of reality belongs only to that which at the same time is necessary: "In the course of its development reality proves to be necessity." A particular governmental measure–Hegel himself cites the example of "a certain tax regulation"–is therefore for him by no means real without qualification. That which is necessary, however, proves itself in the last resort to be also rational; and, applied to the Prussian state of that time, the Hegelian proposition, therefore, merely means: this state is rational, corresponds to reason, insofar as it is necessary; and if it nevertheless appears to us to be evil, but still, in spite of its evil character, continues to exist, then the evil character of the government is justified and explained by the corresponding evil character of its subjects. The Prussians of that day had the government that they deserved.

Now, according to Hegel, reality is, however, in no way an attribute predictable of any given state of affairs, social or political, in all circumstances and at all times. On the contrary. The Roman Republic was real, but so was the Roman Empire, which superseded it. In 1789, the French monarchy had become so unreal, that is to say, so robbed of all necessity, so irrational, that it had to be destroyed by the Great Revolution, of which Hegel always speaks with the greatest enthusiasm. In this case, therefore, the monarchy was the unreal and the revolution the real. And so, in the course of development, all that was previously real becomes unreal, loses it necessity, its right of existence, its rationality. And in the place of moribund reality comes a new, viable reality–peacefully if the old has enough intelligence to go to its death without a struggle; forcibly if it resists this necessity. Thus the Hegelian proposition turns into its opposite through Hegelian dialectics itself: All that is real in the sphere of human history, becomes irrational in the process of time, is therefore irrational by its very destination, is tainted beforehand with irrationality, and everything which is rational in the minds of men is destined to become real, however much it may contradict existing apparent reality. In accordance with all the rules of the Hegelian method of thought, the proposition of the rationality of everything which is real resolves itself into the other proposition: All that exists deserves to perish.

But precisely therein lay the true significance and the revolutionary character of the Hegelian philosophy (to which, as the close of the whole movement since Kant, we must here confine ourselves), that it once and for all dealt the death blow to the finality of all product of human thought and action. Truth, the cognition of which is the business of philosophy, was in the hands of Hegel no longer an aggregate of finished dogmatic statements, which, once discovered, had merely to be learned by heart. Truth lay now in the process of cognition itself, in the long historical development of science, which mounts from lower to ever higher levels of knowledge without ever reaching, by discovering so-called absolute truth, a point at which it can proceed no further, where it would have nothing more to do than to fold its hands and gaze with wonder at the absolute truth to which it had attained. And what holds good for the realm of philosophical knowledge holds good also for that of every other kind of knowledge and also for practical action. Just as knowledge is unable to reach a complete conclusion in a perfect, ideal condition of humanity, so is history unable to do so; a perfect society, a perfect "state", are things which can only exist in imagination. On the contrary, all successive historical systems are only transitory stages in the endless course of development of human society from the lower to the higher. Each stage is necessary, and therefore justified for the time and conditions to which it owes its origin. But in the face of new, higher conditions which gradually develop in its own womb, it loses vitality and justification. It must give way to a higher stage which will also in its turn decay and perish. Just as the bourgeoisie by large-scale industry, competition, and the world market dissolves in practice all stable time-honored institutions, so this dialectical philosophy dissolves all conceptions of final, absolute truth and of absolute states of humanity corresponding to it. For it (dialectical philosophy), nothing is final, absolute, sacred. It reveals the transitory character of everything and in everything; nothing can endure before it except the uninterrupted process of becoming and of passing away, of endless ascendancy from the lower to the higher. And dialectical philosophy itself is nothing more than the mere reflection of this process in the thinking brain. It has, of course, also a conservative side; it recognizes that definite stages of knowledge and society are justified for their time and circumstances; but only so far. The conservatism of this mode of outlook is relative; its revolutionary character is absolute– the only absolute dialectical philosophy admits.

It is not necessary, here, to go into the question of whether this mode of outlook is thoroughly in accord with the present state of natural science, which predicts a possible end even for the Earth, and for its habitability a fairly certain one; which therefore recognizes that for the history of mankind, too, there is not only an ascending but also a descending branch. At any rate, we still find ourselves a considerable distance from the turning-point at which the historical course of society becomes one of descent, and we cannot expect Hegelian philosophy to be concerned with a subject which natural science, in its time, had not at all placed upon the agenda as yet.

But what must, in fact, be said here is this: that in Hegel the views developed above are not so sharply delineated. They are a necessary conclusion from his method, but one which he himself never drew with such explicitness. And this, indeed, for the simple reason that he was compelled to make a system and, in accordance with traditional requirements, a system of philosophy must conclude with some sort of absolute truth. Therefore, however much Hegel, especially in his *Logic*, emphasized that this eternal truth is nothing but the logical, or, the historical, process itself, he nevertheless finds himself compelled to supply this process with an end, just because he has to bring his system to a termination at some point or other. In his *Logic*, he can make this end a beginning again, since here the point of the conclusion, the Absolute Idea–which is only absolute insofar as he has absolutely nothing to say about it–"alienates," that is, transforms, itself into nature and comes to itself again later in the mind, that is, in thought and in history. But at the end of the whole philosophy, a similar return to the beginning is possible only in one way. Namely, by conceiving of the end of history as follows: mankind arrives at the cognition of the self-same Absolute Idea, and declares that this cognition of the Absolute Idea is reached in Hegelian philosophy. In this way, however, the whole dogmatic content of the Hegelian system is declared to be absolute truth, in contradiction to his dialectical method, which dissolves all dogmatism. Thus the revolutionary side is smothered beneath the overgrowth of the conservative side. And what applies to philosophical cognition applies also to historical practice. Mankind, which, in the person of Hegel, has reached the point of working out the Absolute Idea, must also in practice have gotten so far that it can carry out this Absolute Idea in reality. Hence, the practical political demands of the Absolute Idea on contemporaries may not be stretched too far. And so we find at the conclusion of the *Philosophy of Right* that the Absolute Idea is to be realized in that monarchy based on social estates which Frederick William III so persistently but vainly promised to his subjects, that is, in a limited, moderate, indirect rule of the possessing classes suited to the petty-bourgeois German conditions of that time; and, moreover, the necessity of the nobility is demonstrated to us in a speculative fashion.

The inner necessities of the system are, therefore, of themselves sufficient to explain why a thoroughly revolutionary method of thinking produced an extremely tame political conclusion. As a matter of fact, the specific form of this conclusion springs from this, that Hegel was a German, and like his contemporary Goethe had a bit of the philistine's queue dangling behind. Each of them was an Olympian Zeus in his own sphere, yet neither of them ever quite freed himself from German philistinism.

But all this did not prevent the Hegelian system from covering an incomparably greater domain than any earlier system, nor from developing in this domain a wealth of thought, which is astounding even today. The phenomenology of mind (which one may call a parallel of the embryology and paleontology of the mind, a development of individual consciousness through its different stages, set in the form of an abbreviated reproduction of the stages through which the consciousness of man has passed in the course of history), logic, natural philosophy, philosophy of mind, and the latter worked out in its separate, historical subdivisions: philosophy of history, of right, of religion, history of philosophy, aesthetics, etc.–in all these different historical fields Hegel labored to discover and demonstrate the pervading thread of development. And as he was not only a creative genius but also a man of encyclopedic erudition, he played an epoch-making role in every sphere. It is self-evident that owing to the needs of the "system" he very often had to resort to those forced constructions about which his pigmy[6] opponents make such a terrible fuss even today. But these constructions are only the frame and scaffolding of his work. If one does not loiter here needlessly, but presses on farther into the immense building, one finds innumerable treasures which today still possess undiminished value. With all philosophers it is precisely the "system" which is perishable; and for the simple reason that it springs from an imperishable desire of the human mind–the desire to overcome all contradictions. But if all contradictions are once and for all disposed of, we shall have arrived at so-called absolute truth–world history will be at an end. And yet it has to continue, although there is nothing left for it to do–hence, a new, insoluble contradiction. As soon as we have once realized–and in the long run no one has helped us to realize it more than Hegel himself–that the task of philosophy thus stated means nothing but the task that a single philosopher should accomplish that which can only be accomplished by the entire human race in its progressive development–as soon as we realize that, there is an end to all philosophy in the hitherto accepted sense of the word. One leaves alone "absolute truth," which is unattainable along this path or by any single individual; instead, one pursues attainable relative truths along the path of the positive sciences, and the summation of their results by means of dialectical thinking. At any rate, with Hegel philosophy comes to an end; on the one hand, because in his system he summed up its whole development in the most splendid fashion; and on the other hand, because, even though unconsciously, he showed us the way out of the labyrinth of systems to real positive knowledge of the world.

One can imagine what a tremendous effect this Hegelian system must have produced in the philosophy-tinged atmosphere of Germany. It was a triumphant procession which lasted for decades and which by no means came to a standstill on the death of Hegel. On the contrary, it was precisely from 1830 to 1840 that "Hegelianism" reigned most exclusively, and to a greater or lesser extent infected even its opponents. It was precisely in this period that Hegelian views, consciously or unconsciously, most extensively penetrated the most diversified sciences and leavened even popular literature and the daily press, from which the average "educated consciousness" derives its mental pabulum. But this victory along the whole front was only the prelude to an internal struggle.

As we have seen, the doctrine of Hegel, taken as a whole, left plenty of room for giving shelter to the most diverse practical party views. And in the theoretical Germany of that time, two things above all were practical: religion and politics. Whoever placed the chief emphasis on the Hegelian *system* could be fairly conservative in both spheres; whoever regarded the dialectical *method* as the main thing could belong to the most extreme opposition, both in politics and religion. Hegel himself, despite the fairly frequent outbursts of revolutionary wrath in his works, seemed on the whole to be more inclined to the conservative side. Indeed, his system had cost him much more "hard mental plugging" than his method. Towards the end of the thirties, the cleavage in the school became more and more apparent. The Left wing, the so-called Young Hegelians, in their fight with the pietist orthodox and the feudal reactionaries, abandoned bit by bit that philosophical-genteel reserve in regard to the burning questions of the day which up to that time had secured state toleration and even protection for their teachings. And when in 1840, orthodox pietism and absolutist feudal reaction ascended the throne with Frederick William IV, open partisanship became unavoidable. The fight was still carried on with philosophical weapons, but no longer for abstract philosophical aims. It turned directly on the destruction of traditional religion and of the existing state. And while in the *Deutsche Jahrbucher* the practical ends were still predominantly put forward in philosophical disguise, in the *Rheinische Zeitung* of 1842 the Young Hegelian school revealed itself directly as the philosophy of the aspiring radical bourgeoisie and used the meager cloak of philosophy only to deceive the censorship.

At that time, however, politics was a very thorny field, and hence the main fight came to be directed against religion; this fight, particularly since 1840, was indirectly also political. Sjtrauss' *Life of Jesus*, published in 1835, had provided the first impulse. The theory therein developed of the formation of the gospel myths was combated later by Bruno Bauer with proof that a whole series of evangelic stories had been fabricated by the authors themselves. The controversy between these two was carried out in the philosophical disguise of a battle between "self-consciousness" and "substance." The question whether the miracle stories of the gospels came into being through unconscious-traditional myth-creation within the bosom of the community or whether they were fabricated by the

41

evangelists themselves was magnified into the question whether, in world history, "substance" or "self-consciousness" was the decisive operative force. Finally came Stirner, the prophet of contemporary anarchism–Bakunin has taken a great deal from him–and capped the sovereign "self-consciousness" by his sovereign "ego."

We will not go further into this side of the decomposition process of the Hegelian school. More important for us is the following: the main body of the most determined Young Hegelians was, by the practical necessities of its fight against positive religion, driven back to Anglo-French materialism. This brought them into conflict with the system of their school. While materialism conceives nature as the sole reality, nature in the Hegelian system represents merely the "alienation" of the Absolute Idea, so to say, a degradation of the idea. At all events, thinking and its thought-product, the idea, is here the primary, nature the derivative, which only exists at all by the condescension of the idea. And in this contradiction they floundered as well or as ill as they could.

Then came Feuerbach's *Essence of Christianity*. With one blow, it pulverized the contradiction, in that without circumlocutions it placed materialism on the throne again. Nature exists independently of all philosophy. It is the foundation upon which we human beings, ourselves products of nature, have grown up. Nothing exists outside nature and man, and the higher beings our religious fantasies have created are only the fantastic reflection of our own essence. The spell was broken; the "system" was exploded and cast aside, and the contradiction, shown to exist only in our imagination, was dissolved. One must himself have experienced the liberating effect of this book to get an idea of it. Enthusiasm was general; we all became at once Feuerbachians. How enthusiastically Marx greeted the new conception and how much–in spite of all critical reservations–he was influenced by it, one may read in the *The Holy Family*.

Even the shortcomings of the book contributed to its immediate effect. Its literary, sometimes even high-flown, style secured for it a large public and was at any rate refreshing after long years of abstract and abstruse Hegelianizing. The same is true of its extravagant deification of love, which, coming after the now intolerable sovereign rule of "pure reason," had its excuse, if not justification. But what we must not forget is that it was precisely these two weaknesses of Feuerbach that "true Socialism," which had been spreading like a plague in educated Germany since 1844, took as its starting-point, putting literary phrases in the place of scientific knowledge, the liberation of mankind by means of "love" in place of the emancipation of the proletariat through the economic transformation of production–in short, losing itself in the nauseous fine writing and ecstasies of love typified by Herr Karl Grun.

Another thing we must not forget is this: the Hegelian school disintegrated, but Hegelian philosophy was not overcome through criticism; Strauss and Bauer each took one of its sides and set it polemically against the other. Feuerbach smashed the system and simply discarded it. But a philosophy is not disposed of by the mere assertion that it is false. And so powerful a work as Hegelian philosophy, which had exercised so enormous an influence on the intellectual development of the nation, could not be disposed of by simply being ignored. It had to be "sublated" in its own sense, that is, in the sense that while its form had to be annihilated through criticism, the new content which had been won through it had to be saved. How this was brought about we shall see below.

43

But in the meantime, the Revolution of 1848 thrust the whole of philosophy aside as unceremoniously as Feuerbach had thrust aside Hegel. And in the process, Feuerbach himself was also pushed into the background.

Materialism

The great basic question of all philosophy, especially of more recent philosophy, is that concerning the relation of thinking and being. From the very early times when men, still completely ignorant of the structure of their own bodies, under the stimulus of dream apparitions[7] came to believe that their thinking and sensation were not activities of their bodies, but of a distinct soul which inhabits the body and leaves it at death–from this time men have been driven to reflect about the relation between this soul and the outside world. If, upon death, it took leave of the body and lived on, there was no occasion to invent yet another distinct death for it. Thus arose the idea of immortality, which at that stage of development appeared not at all as a consolation but as a fate against which it was no use fighting, and often enough, as among the Greeks, as a positive misfortune. The quandary arising from the common universal ignorance of what to do with this soul, once its existence had been accepted, after the death of the body, and not religious desire for consolation, led in a general way to the tedious notion of personal immortality. In an exactly similar manner, the first gods arose through the personification of natural forces. And these gods in the further development of religions assumed more and more extramundane form, until finally by a process of abstraction, I might almost say of distillation, occurring naturally in the course of man's intellectual development, out of the many more or less limited and mutually limiting gods there arose in the minds of men the idea of the one exclusive God of the monotheistic religions.

Thus the question of the relation of thinking to being, the relation of the spirit to nature–the paramount question of the whole of philosophy–has, no less than all religion, its roots in the narrow-minded and ignorant notions of savagery. But this question could for the first time be put forward in its whole acuteness, could achieve its full significance, only after humanity in Europe had awakened from the long hibernation of the Christian Middle Ages. The question of the position of thinking in relation to being, a question which, by the way, had played a great part also in the scholasticism of the Middle Ages, the question: which is primary, spirit or nature–that question, in relation to the church, was sharpened into this: Did God create the world or has the world been in existence eternally?

The answers which the philosophers gave to this question split them into two great camps. Those who asserted the primacy of spirit to nature and, therefore, in the last instance, assumed world creation in some form or other–and among the philosophers, Hegel, for example, this creation often becomes still more intricate and impossible than in Christianity–comprised the camp of idealism. The others, who regarded nature as primary, belong to the various schools of materialism.

These two expressions, idealism and materialism, originally signify nothing else but this; and here too they are not used in any other sense. What confusion arises when some other meaning is put to them will be seen below.

But the question of the relation of thinking and being had yet another side: in what relation do our thoughts about the world surrounding us stand to this world itself? Is our thinking capable of the cognition of the real world? Are we able in our ideas and notions of the real world to produce a correct reflection of reality? In philosophical language this question is called the question of identity of thinking and being, and the overwhelming majority of philosophers give an affirmative answer to this question. With Hegel, for example, its affirmation is

46

self-evident; for what we cognize in the real world is precisely its thought-content–that which makes the world a gradual realization of the Absolute Idea, which Absolute Idea has existed somewhere from eternity, independent of the world and before the world. But it is manifest without further proof that thought can know a content which is from the outset a thought-content. It is equally manifest that what is to be proved here is already tacitly contained in the premises. But that in no way prevents Hegel from drawing the further conclusion from his proof of the identity of thinking and being that his philosophy, because it is correct for his thinking, is therefore the only correct one, and that the identity of thinking and being must prove its validity by mankind immediately translating his philosophy from theory into practice and transforming the whole world according to Hegelian principles. This is an illusion which he shares with well-nigh all philosophers.

In addition, there is yet a set of different philosophers–those who question the possibility of any cognition, or at least of an exhaustive cognition, of the world. To them, among the more modern ones, belong Hume and Kant, and they played a very important role in philosophical development. What is decisive in the refutation of this view has already been said by Hegel, in so far as this was possible from an idealist standpoint. The materialistic additions made by Feuerbach are more ingenious than profound. The most telling refutation of this as of all other philosophical crotchets is practice–namely, experiment and industry. If we are able to prove the correctness of our conception of a natural process by making it ourselves, bringing it into being out of its conditions and making it serve our own purposes into the bargain, then there is an end to the Kantian ungraspable "thing-in-itself." The chemical substances produced in the bodies of plants and animals remained just such "things-in-themselves" until organic chemistry began to produce them one after another, whereupon the "thing-in-itself" became a thing for us–as, for instance, alizarin, the coloring matter of the madder plant, which we no longer trouble to grow in the madder roots in the field, but produce much more cheaply and simply from coal tar. For 300 years, the Copernican solar system was a hypothesis with 100, 1,000, 10,000 to 1 chances in its favor, but still always a hypothesis. But then Leverrier, by means of the data provided by this system, not only deduced the necessity of the existence of an unknown planet, but also calculated the position in the heavens which this planet must necessarily occupy, and when Johann Galle really found this planet (Neptune, discovered 1846, at Berlin Observatory), the Copernican system was proved. If, nevertheless, the neo-Kantians are attempting to resurrect the Kantian conception in Germany, and the agnostics that of Hume in England (where in fact it never became extinct), this is, in view of their theoretical and practical refutation accomplished long ago, scientifically a regression and practically merely a shamefaced way of surreptitiously accepting materialism, while denying it before the world.

But during this long period from Descartes to Hegel and from Hobbes to Feuerbach, these philosophers were by no means impelled, as they thought they were, solely by the force of pure reason. On the contrary, what really pushed them forward most was the powerful and ever more rapidly onrushing progress of natural science and industry. Among the materialists this was plain on the surface, but the idealist systems also filled themselves more and more with a materialist content and attempted pantheistically to reconcile the antithesis between mind and matter. Thus, ultimately, the Hegelian system represents merely a materialism idealistically turned upside down in method and content.

It is, therefore, comprehensible that Starcke in his characterization of Feuerbach first of all investigates the latter's position in regard to this fundamental question of the relation of thinking and being. After a short introduction, in which the views of the preceding philosophers, particularly since Kant, are described in unnecessarily ponderous philosophical language, and in which Hegel, by an all too formalistic adherence to certain passages of his works, gets far less his due, there follows a detailed description of the course of development of Feuerbach's "metaphysics" itself, as this course was successively reflected in those writings of this philosopher which have a bearing here. This description is industriously and lucidly elaborated; only, like the whole book, it is loaded with a ballast of philosophical phraseology by no means everywhere unavoidable, which is the more disturbing in its effect the less the author keeps to the manner of expression of one and the same school, or even of Feuerbach himself, and the more he interjects expressions of very different tendencies, especially of the tendencies now rampant and calling themselves philosophical.

The course of evolution of Feuerbach is that of a Hegelian–a never quite orthodox Hegelian, it is true–into a materialist; an evolution which at a definite stage necessitates a complete rupture with the idealist system of his predecessor. With irresistible force, Feuerbach is finally driven to the realization that the Hegelian pre-mundane existence of the "Absolute Idea," the "pre-existence of the logical categories" before the world existed, is nothing more than the fantastic survival of the belief in the existence of an extra-mundane creator; that the material, sensuously perceptible world to which we ourselves belong is the only reality; and that our consciousness and thinking, however super-sensuous they may seem, are the product of a material, bodily organ, the brain. Matter is not a product of mind, but mind itself is merely the highest product of matter. This is, of course, pure materialism. But, having got so far, Feuerbach stops short. He cannot overcome the customary philosophical prejudice, prejudice not against the thing but against the name materialism. He says:

> "To me materialism is the foundation of the edifice of human essence and knowledge; but to me it is not what it is to the physiologist, to the natural scientists in the narrower sense, for example, to Moleschott, and necessarily is from their standpoint and profession, namely, the edifice itself. Backwards I fully agree with the materialists; but not forwards."

Here, Feuerbach lumps together the materialism that is a general world outlook resting upon a definite conception of the relation between matter and mind, and the special form in which this world outlook was expressed at a definite historical stage–namely, in the 18th century. More than that, he lumps it with the shallow, vulgarized form in which the materialism of the 18th century continues to exist today in the heads of naturalists and physicians, the form which was preached on their tours in the fifties by Buchner, Vogt, and Moleschott. But just as idealism underwent a series of stages of development, so also did materialism. With each epoch-making discovery even in the sphere of natural science, it has to change its form; and after history was also subjected to materialistic treatment, a new avenue of development has opened here, too.

The materialism of the last century was predominantly mechanical, because at that time, of all natural sciences, only mechanics, and indeed only the mechanics of solid bodies–celestial and terrestrial–in short, the mechanics of gravity, had come to any definite close. Chemistry at that time existed only in its infantile, phlogistic form. Biology still lay in swaddling clothes; vegetable and animal organisms had been only roughly examined and were explained by purely mechanical causes. What the animal was to Descartes, man was to the materialists of the 18th century–a machine. This exclusive application of the standards of mechanics to processes of a chemical and organic nature–in which processes the laws of mechanics are, indeed, also valid, but are pushed into the backgrounds by other, higher laws–constitutes the first specific but at that time inevitable limitations of classical French materialism.

The second specific limitation of this materialism lay in its inability to comprehend the universe as a process, as matter undergoing uninterrupted historical development. This was in accordance with the level of the natural science of that time, and with the metaphysical, that is, anti-dialectical manner of philosophizing connected with it. Nature, so much was known, was in eternal motion. But according to the ideas of that time, this motion turned, also eternally, in a circle and therefore never moved from the spot; it produced the same results over and over again. This conception was at that time inevitable. The Kantian theory of the origin of the Solar System (that the Sun and planets originated from incandescent rotating nebulous masses) had been put forward but recently and was still regarded merely as a curiosity. The history of the development of the Earth, geology, was still totally unknown, and the conception that the animate natural beings of today are the result of a long sequence of development from the simple to the complex could not at that time scientifically be put forward at all. The unhistorical view of nature was therefore inevitable. We have little reason to reproach the philosophers of the 18th century on this account since the same thing is found in Hegel. According to him, nature, as a mere "alienation" of the idea, is incapable of development in time–capable only of extending its manifoldness in space, so that it displays simultaneously and alongside of one another all the stages of development comprised in it, and is condemned to an eternal repetition of the same processes. This absurdity of a development in space, but outside of time–the fundamental condition of all development–Hegel imposes upon nature just at the very time when geology, embryology, the physiology of plants and animals, and organic chemistry were being built up, and when everywhere on the basis of these new sciences brilliant foreshadowing of the later theory of evolution were appearing (for instance, Goethe and Lamarck). But the system demanded it; hence the method, for the sake of the system, had to become untrue to itself.

This same unhistorical conception prevailed also in the domain of history. Here the struggle against the remnants of the Middle Ages blurred the view. The Middle Ages were regarded as a mere interruption of history by a thousand years of universal barbarism. The great progress made in the Middle Ages–the extension of the area of European culture, the viable great nations taking form there next to each other, and finally the enormous technical progress of the 14th and 15th centuries–all this was not seen. Thus a rational insight into the great historical interconnectedness was made impossible, and history served at best as a collection of examples and illustrations for the use of philosophers.

The vulgarizing peddlers, who in Germany in the fifties dabbled in materialism, by no means overcame this limitation of their teachers. All the advances of natural science which had been made in the meantime served them only as new proofs against the existence of a creator of the world; and, indeed, they did not in the least make it their business to develop the theory any further. Though idealism was at the end of its tether and was dealt a death-blow by the Revolution of 1848, it had the satisfaction of seeing that materialism had for the moment fallen lower still. Feuerbach was unquestionably right when he refused to take responsibility for this materialism; only he should not have confounded the doctrines of these itinerant preachers with materialism in general.

Here, however, there are two things to be pointed out. First, even during Feuerbach's lifetime, natural science was still in that process of violent fermentation which only during the last 15 years had reached a clarifying, relative conclusion. New scientific data were acquired to a hitherto unheard of extent, but the establishing of interrelations, and thereby the bringing of order into this chaos of discoveries following closely upon each other's heels, has only quite recently become possible. It is true that Feuerbach had lived to see all three of the decisive discoveries–that of the cell, the transformation of energy, and the theory of evolution named after Darwin. But how could the lonely philosopher, living in rural solitude, be able sufficiently to follow scientific developments in order to appreciate at their full value discoveries which natural scientists themselves at that time either still contested or did not know how to make adequate use of? The blame for this falls solely upon the wretched conditions in Germany, in consequence of which cobweb-spinning eclectic flea-crackers had taken possession of the chairs of philosophy, while Feuerbach, who towered above them all, had to rusticate and grow sour in a little village. It is therefore not Feuerbach's fault that this historical conception of nature, which had now become possible and which removed all the onesidedness of French materialism, remained inaccessible to him.

Secondly, Feuerbach is quite correct in asserting that exclusively natural-scientific materialism is indeed "the foundation of the edifice of human knowledge, but not the edifice itself." For we live not only in nature but also in human society, and this also no less than nature has its history of development and its science. It was therefore a question of bringing the science of society, that is, the sum total of the so-called historical and philosophical sciences, into harmony with the materialist foundation, and of reconstructing it thereupon. But it did not fall to Feuerbach's lot to do this. In spite of the "foundation," he remained here bound by the traditional idealist fetters, a fact which he recognizes in these words: "Backwards I agree with the materialists, but not forwards!"

But it was Feuerbach himself who did not go "forwards" here; in the social domain, who did not get beyond his standpoint of 1840 or 1844. And this was again chiefly due to this reclusion which compelled him, who, of all philosophers, was the most inclined to social intercourse, to produce thoughts out of his solitary head instead of in amicable and hostile encounters with other men of his calibre. Later, we shall see in detail how much he remained an idealist in this sphere.

It need only be added here that Starcke looks for Feuerbach's idealism in the wrong place.

"Feuerbach is an idealist; he believes in the progress of mankind." (p.19)

"The foundation, the substructure of the whole, remains nevertheless idealism. Realism for us is nothing more than a protection again aberrations, while we follow our ideal trends. Are not compassion, love, and enthusiasm for truth and justice ideal forces?" (p.VIII)

In the first place, idealism here means nothing, but the pursuit of ideal aims. But these necessarily have to do at the most with Kantian idealism and its "categorical imperative"; however, Kant himself called his philosophy "Transcendental Idealism" by no means because he dealt therein also with ethical ideals, but for quite other reasons, as Starcke will remember. The superstition that philosophical idealism is pivoted round a belief in ethical, that is, social, ideals, arose outside philosophy, among the German philistines, who learned by heart from Schiller's poems the few morsels of philosophical culture they needed. No one has criticized more severely the impotent "categorical imperative" of Kant–impotent because it demands the impossible, and therefore never attains to any reality–no one has more cruelly derided the philistine sentimental enthusiasm for unrealizable ideals purveyed by Schiller than precisely the complete idealist Hegel (see, for example, his *Phenomenology of Spirit*).

In the second place, we simply cannot get away from the fact that everything that sets men acting must find its way through their brains–even eating and drinking, which begins as a consequence of the sensation of hunger or thirst transmitted through the brain, and ends as a result of the sensation of satisfaction likewise transmitted through the brain. The influences of the external world upon man express themselves in his brain, are reflected therein as feelings, impulses, volitions–in short, as "ideal tendencies," and in this form become "ideal powers." If, then, a man is to be deemed an idealist because he

55

follows "ideal tendencies" and admits that "ideal powers" have an influence over him, then every person who is at all normally developed is a born idealist and how, in that case, can there still be any materialists?

In the third place, the conviction that humanity, at least at the present moment, moves on the whole in a progressive direction has absolutely nothing to do with the antagonism between materialism and idealism. The French materialists no less than the deists Voltaire and Rousseau held this conviction to an almost fanatical degree, and often enough made the greatest personal sacrifices for it. If ever anybody dedicated his whole life to the "enthusiasm for truth and justice"–using this phrase in the good sense–it was Diderot, for instance. If, therefore, Starcke declares all this to be idealism, this merely proves that the word materialism, and the whole antagonism between the two trends, has lost all meaning for him here.

The fact is that Starcke, although perhaps unconsciously, in this makes an unpardonable concession to the traditional philistine prejudice against the word materialism resulting from its long-continued defamation by the priests. By the word materialism, the philistine understands gluttony, drunkenness, lust of the eye, lust of the flesh, arrogance, cupidity, avarice, covetousness, profit-hunting, and stock-exchange swindling–in short, all the filthy vices in which he himself indulges in private. By the word idealism he understands the belief in virtue, universal philanthropy, and in a general way a "better world," of which he boasts before others but in which he himself at the utmost believes only so long as he is having the blues or is going through the bankruptcy consequent upon his customary "materialist" excesses. It is then that he sings his favorite song, What is man?–Half beast, half angel.

For the rest, Starcke takes great pains to defend Feuerbach against the attacks and doctrines of the vociferous assistant professors who today go by the name of philosophers in Germany. For people who are interested in this afterbirth of classical German philosophy this is, of course, a matter of importance; for Starcke himself it may have appeared necessary. We, however, will spare the reader this.

Feuerbach

The real idealism of Feuerbach becomes evident as soon as we come to his philosophy of religion and ethics. He by no means wishes to abolish religion; he wants to perfect it. Philosophy itself must be absorbed in religion.

"The periods of humanity are distinguished only by religious changes. A historical movement is fundamental only when it is rooted in the hearts of men. The heart is not a form of religion, so that the latter should exist *also* in the heart; the heart is the essence of religion." (Quoted by Starcke, p.168.)

According to Feuerbach, religion is the relation between human beings based on the affections, the relation based on the heart, which relation until now has sought its truth in a fantastic mirror image of reality—in the mediation of one or many gods, the fantastic mirror images of human qualities—but now finds it directly and without any mediation in the love between "I" and "Thou." Thus, finally, with Feuerbach sexual love becomes one of the highest forms, if not the highest form, of the practice of his new religion.

Now relations between human beings, based on affection, and especially between the two sexes, have existed as long as mankind has. Sexual love in particular has undergone a development and won a place during the last 800 years which has made it a compulsory pivotal point of all poetry during this period. The existing positive religions have limited themselves to the bestowal of a higher consecration upon state-regulated sexual love—that is, upon the marriage laws—and they could all disappear tomorrow without changing in the slightest the practice of love and friendship. Thus the Christian religion in France, as a matter of fact, so completely disappeared in the year 1793–95 that even Napoleon could not reintroduce it without opposition and difficulty; and this without any need for a substitute in Feuerbach's sense, making itself in the interval.

Feuerbach's idealism consists here in this: he does not simply accept mutual relations based on reciprocal inclination between human beings, such as sexual love, friendship, compassion, self-sacrifice, etc., as what they are in themselves–without associating them with any particular religion which to him, too, belongs to the past; but instead he asserts that they will attain their full value only when consecrated by the name of religion. The chief thing for him is not that these purely human relations exist, but that they shall be conceived of as the new, true, religion. They are to have full value only after they have been marked with a religious stamp. Religion is derived from *religare* ("to bind") and meant, originally, a bond. Therefore, every bond between two people is a religion. Such etymological tricks are the last resort of idealist philosophy. Not what the word means according to the historical development of its actual use, but what it ought to mean according to its derivation is what counts. And so sexual love, and the intercourse between the sexes, is apotheosized to a *religion*, merely in order that the word religion, which is so dear to idealistic memories, may not disappear from the language. The Parisian reformers of the Louis Blanc trend used to speak in precisely the same way in the forties. They, likewise, could conceive of a man without religion only as a monster, and used to say to us: "*Donc, l'atheisme c'est votre religion!*" ("Well, then atheism is your religion!") If Feuerbach wishes to establish a true religion upon the basis of an essentially materialist conception of nature, that is the same as regarding modern chemistry as true alchemy. If religion can exist without its god, alchemy can exist without its philosopher's stone. By the way, there exists a very close connection between alchemy and religion. The philosopher's stone has many godlike properties and the Egyptian-Greek alchemists of the first two centuries of our era had a hand in the development of Christian doctrines, as the data given by Kopp and Bertholet have proved.

Feuerbach's assertion that "the periods of humanity are distinguished only by religious changes" is decidedly false. Great historical turning-points have been *accompanied* by religious changes only so far as the three world religions which have existed up to the present–Buddhism, Christianity, and Islam–are concerned. The old tribal and national religions, which arose spontaneously, did not proselytize and lost all their power of resistance as soon as the independence of the tribe or people was lost. For the Germans, it was sufficient to have simple contact with the decaying Roman world empire and with its newly adopted Christian world religion which fitted its economic, political, and ideological conditions. Only with these world religions, arisen more or less artificially, particularly Christianity and Islam, do we find that the more general historical movements acquire a religious imprint. Even in regard to Christianity, the religious stamp in revolutions of really universal significance is restricted to the first stages of the bourgeoisie's struggle for emancipation–from the 13th to the 17th century–and is to be accounted for, not as Feuerbach thinks by the hearts of men and their religious needs, but by the entire previous history of the Middle Ages, which knew no other form of ideology than religion and theology. But when the bourgeoisie of the 18th century was strengthened enough likewise to posses an ideology of its own, suited to its own class standpoint, it made its great and conclusive revolution–the French,–appealing exclusively to juristic and political ideas, and troubling itself with religion only in so far as it stood in its way. But it never occurred to it to put a new religion in place of the old. Everyone knows how Robespierre failed in his attempt (to set up a religion of the "highest being").

The possibility of purely human sentiments in our intercourse with other human beings has nowadays been sufficiently curtailed by the society in which we must live, which is based upon class antagonism and class rule. We have no reason to curtail it more still by exalting these sentiments to a religion. And similarly the understanding of the great historical class struggles has already been sufficiently obscured by current historiography, particularly in Germany, so that there is also no need for us to make such an understanding totally impossible by transforming the history of these struggles into a mere appendix of ecclesiastical history. Already here it becomes evident how far today we have moved beyond Feuerbach. His "finest" passages in glorification of his new religion of love are totally unreadable today.

The only religion which Feuerbach examines seriously is Christianity, the world religion of the Occident,[8] based upon monotheism. He proves that the Christian god is only a fantastic reflection, a mirror image, of man. Now, this god is, however, himself the product of a tedious process of abstraction, the concentrated quintessence of the numerous earlier tribal and national gods. And man, whose image this god is, is therefore also not a real man, but likewise the quintessence of the numerous real men, man in the abstract, therefore himself again a mental image. Feuerbach, who on every page preaches sensuousness, absorption in the concrete, in actuality, becomes thoroughly abstract as soon as he begins to talk of any other than mere sex relations between human beings.

Of these relations, only one aspect appeals to him: morality. And here we are again struck by Feuerbach's astonishing poverty when compared to Hegel. The latter's ethics, or doctrine of moral conduct, is the philosophy of right, and embraces: (1) abstract right; (2) morality; (3) social ethics [Sittlichkeit], under which are comprised: the family, civil society, and the state.

Here the content is as realistic as the form is idealistic. Besides morality, the whole sphere of law, economy, politics is here included. With Feuerbach, it is just the reverse. In the form he is realistic since he takes his start from man; but there is absolutely no mention of the world in which this man lives; hence, this man remains always the same abstract man who occupied the field in the philosophy of religion. For this man is not born of woman; he issues, as from a chrysalis, from the god of monotheistic religions. He therefore does not live in a real world historically come into being and historically determined. True, he has intercourse with other men; however, each one of them is just as much an abstraction as he himself. In his philosophy of religion we still had men and women, but in his ethics even this last distinction disappears. Feuerbach, to be sure, at long intervals makes such statements as: "Man thinks differently in a palace and in a hut." "If because of hunger, of misery, you have no stuff in your body, you likewise have no stuff for morality in your head, in your mind, or heart." "Politics must become our religion," etc.

But Feuerbach is absolutely incapable of achieving anything with these maxims. They remain mere phrases, and even Starcke has to admit that for Feuerbach politics constituted an impassable frontier and the "science of society, sociology, was *terra incognita*[9] to him."

He appears just as shallow, in comparison with Hegel, in his treatment of the antithesis of good and evil.

"One believes one is saying something great," Hegel remarks, "if one says that 'man is naturally good.' But one forgets that one says something far greater when one says 'man is naturally evil.'"

With Hegel, evil is the form in which the motive force of historical development presents itself. This contains the twofold meaning that, on the one hand, each new advance necessarily appears as a sacrilege against things hallowed, as a rebellion against condition, though old and moribund, yet sanctified by custom; and that, on the other hand, it is precisely the wicked passions of man–greed and lust for power–which, since the emergence of class antagonisms, serve as levers of historical development–a fact of which the history of feudalism and of the bourgeoisie, for example, constitutes a single continual proof. But it does not occur to Feuerbach to investigate the historical role of moral evil. To him, history is altogether an uncanny domain in which he feels ill at ease. Even his dictum: "Man as he sprang originally from nature was only a mere creature of nature, not a man. Man is a product of man, of culture, of history"–with him, even this dictum remains absolutely sterile.

What Feuerbach has to tell us about morals can, therefore, only be extremely meagre. The urge towards happiness is innate in man, and must therefore form the basis of all morality. But the urge towards happiness is subject to a double correction. First, by the natural consequences of our actions: after the debauching comes the "blues," and habitual excess is followed by illness. Secondly, by its social consequences: if we do not respect the similar urge of other people towards happiness they will defend themselves, and so interfere with our own urge toward happiness. Consequently, in order to satisfy our urge, we must be in a position to appreciate rightly the results of our conduct and must likewise allow others an equal right to seek happiness. Rational self-restraint with regard to ourselves, and love—again and again love!—in our intercourse with others—these are the basic laws of Feuerbach's morality; from them, all others are derived. And neither the most spirited utterances of Feuerbach nor the strongest eulogies of Starcke can hide the tenuity and banality of these few propositions.

Only very exceptionally, and by no means to this and other people's profit, can an individual satisfy his urge towards happiness by preoccupation with himself. Rather, it requires preoccupation with the outside world, with means to satisfy his needs—that is to say, food, an individual of the opposite sex, books, conversation, argument, activities, objects for use and working up. Feuerbach's morality either presupposes that these means and objects of satisfaction are given to every individual as a matter of course, or else it offers only inapplicable good advice and is, therefore, not worth a brass farthing to people who are without these means. And Feuerbach himself states this in plain terms:

"Man thinks differently in a palace and in a hut. If because of hunger, of misery, you have no stuff in your body, you likewise have no stuff for morality in your head, in your mind, or heart."

Do matters fare any better in regard to the equal right of others to satisfy their urge towards happiness? Feuerbach posed this claim as absolute, as holding good for all times and circumstances. But since when has it been valid? Was there ever in antiquity between slaves and masters, or in the Middle Ages between serfs and barons, any talk about an equal right to the urge towards happiness? Was not the urge towards happiness of the oppressed class sacrificed ruthlessly and "by the right of law" to that of the ruling class? Yes, that was indeed immoral; nowadays, however, equality of rights is recognized. Recognized in words ever since and inasmuch as the bourgeoisie, in its fight against feudalism and in the development of capitalist production, was compelled to abolish all privileges of estate, that is, personal privileges, and to introduce the equality of all individuals before law, first in the sphere in private law, then gradually also in the sphere of public law. But the urge towards happiness thrives only to a trivial extent on ideal rights. To the greatest extent of all it thrives on material means; and capitalist production takes care to ensure that the great majority of those equal rights shall get only what is essential for bare existence. Capitalist production has, therefore, little more respect, if indeed any more, for the equal right to the urge towards happiness of the majority than had slavery or serfdom. And are we better off in regard to the mental means of happiness, the educational means? Is not even "the schoolmaster of Sadowa"[10] a mythical person?

According to Feuerbach's theory of morals, the Stock Exchange is the highest temple of moral conduct, provided only that one always speculates right. If my urge towards happiness leads me to the Stock Exchange, and if there I correctly gauge the consequences of my actions so that only agreeable results and no disadvantages ensue–that is, I always win–then I am fulfilling Feuerbach's precept. Moreover, I do not thereby interfere with the equal right of another person to pursue his happiness; for that other man went to the Stock Exchange just as voluntarily as I did and in concluding the speculative transaction with me he has followed his urge towards happiness as I have followed mine. If he loses his money, his action is *ipso facto* proved to have been unethical, because of his bad reckoning, and since I have given him the punishment he deserves, I can even slap my chest proudly, like a modern Rhadamanthus.[11] Love, too, rules on the Stock Exchange, in so far as it is not simply a sentimental figure of speech, for each finds in others the satisfaction of his own urge towards happiness, which is just what love ought to achieve and how it acts in practice. And if I gamble with correct prevision of the consequences of my operations, and therefore with success, I fulfill all the strictest injunctions of Feuerbachian morality–and becomes a rich man into the bargain. In other words, Feuerbach's morality is cut exactly to the pattern of modern capitalist society, little as Feuerbach himself might desire or imagine it.

But love!–yes, with Feuerbach, love is everywhere and at all times the wonder-working god who should help to surmount all difficulties of practical life–and at that in a society which is split into classes with diametrically opposite interests. At this point, the last relic of the revolutionary character disappears from his philosophy, leaving only the old cant: Love one another–fall into each other's arms regardless of distinctions of sex or estate–a universal orgy of reconciliation!

In short, the Feuerbachian theory of morals fares like all its predecessors. It is designed to suit all periods, all peoples and all conditions, and precisely for that reason it is never and nowhere applicable. It remains, as regards the real world, as powerless as Kant's categorical imperative. In reality every class, even every profession, has its own morality, and even this it violates whenever it can do so with impunity. And love, which is to unite all, manifests itself in wars, altercations, lawsuits, domestic broils, divorces, and every possible exploitation of one by another.

Now how was it possible that the powerful impetus given by Feuerbach turned out to be so unfruitful for himself? For the simple reason that Feuerbach himself never contrives to escape from the realm of abstraction–for which he has a deadly hatred–into that of living reality. He clings fiercely to nature and man; but nature and man remain mere words with him. He is incapable of telling us anything definite either about real nature or real men. But from the abstract man of Feuerbach, one arrives at real living men only when one considers them as participants in history. And that is what Feuerbach resisted, and therefore the year 1848, which he did not understand, meant to him merely the final break with the real world, retirement into solitude. The blame for this again falls chiefly on the conditions them obtaining in Germany, which condemned him to rot away miserably.

But the step which Feuerbach did not take nevertheless had to be taken. The cult of abstract man, which formed the kernel of Feuerbach's new religion, had to be replaced by the science of real men and of their historical development. This further development of Feuerbach's standpoint beyond Feuerbach was inaugurated by Marx in 1845 in *The Holy Family*.

Marx

Strauss, Bauer, Stirner, Feuerbach–these were the offshoots of Hegelian philosophy, in so far as they did not abandon the field of philosophy. Strauss, after his *Life of Jesus* and *Dogmatics*, produced only literary studies in philosophy and ecclesiastical history after the fashion of Renan. Bauer only achieved something in the field of the history of the origin of Christianity, though what he did here was important. Stirner remained a curiosity, even after Bakunin blended him with Proudhon and labelled the blend "anarchism." Feuerbach alone was of significance as a philosopher. But not only did philosophy–which was claimed to soar above all special sciences and to be the science of sciences connecting them–remain to him an impassable barrier, an inviolable holy thing, but as a philosopher, too, he stopped half-incapable of disposing of Hegel through criticism; he simply threw him aside as useless, while he himself, compared with the encyclopedic wealth of the Hegelian system, achieved nothing positive beyond a turgid religion of love and a meagre, impotent morality.

Out of the dissolution of the Hegelian school, however, there developed still another tendency, the only one which has borne real fruit. And this tendency is essentially connected with the name of Marx.[12]

The separation from Hegelian philosophy was here. Also, the result of a return to the materialist standpoint. That means it was resolved to comprehend the real world–nature and history–just as it presents itself to everyone who approaches it free from preconceived idealist crotchets. It was decided mercilessly to sacrifice every idealist fancy which could not be brought into harmony with the facts conceived in their own and not in a fantastic interconnection. And materialism means nothing more than this. But here the materialistic world outlook was taken very seriously for the first time and was carried through consistently–at least in its basic features–in all domains of knowledge concerned.

Hegel was not simply put aside. On the contrary, a start was made from his revolutionary side, described above, from the dialectical method. But in its Hegelian form, this method was unusable. According to Hegel, dialectics is the self-development of the concept. The absolute concept does not only exist–unknown where–from eternity, it is also the actual living soul of the whole existing world. It develops into itself through all the preliminary stages which are treated at length in the *Logic* and which are all included in it. Then it "alienates" itself by changing into nature, where, unconscious of itself, disguised as a natural necessity, it goes through a new development and finally returns as man's consciousness of himself. This self-consciousness then elaborates itself again in history in the crude form until finally the absolute concept again comes to itself completely in the Hegelian philosophy. According to Hegel, therefore, the dialectical development apparent in nature and history–that is, the causal interconnection of the progressive movement from the lower to the higher, which asserts itself through all zigzag movements and temporary retrogression–is only a poor imitation of the self-movement of the concept going on from eternity, no one knows where, but at all events independently of any thinking human brain. This ideological perversion had to be done away with. We again took a materialistic view of the thoughts in our heads, regarding them as images of real things instead of regarding real things as images of this or that stage of the absolute concept. Thus dialectics reduced itself to the science of the general laws of motion, both of the external world and of human thought–two sets of laws which are identical in substance, but differ in their expression in so far as the human mind can apply them consciously, while in nature and also up to now for the most part in human history, these laws assert themselves unconsciously, in the form of external necessity, in the midst of an endless series of seeming accidents. Thereby the dialectic of concepts itself became merely the conscious reflex of the dialectical motion of the real world and thus the dialectic of Hegel was turned over; or rather, turned off its head, on which it was standing, and placed upon its feet. And this materialist dialectic, which for years has been our best working tool and our sharpest weapon, was, remarkably enough, discovered not only by us but also, independently of us and even of Hegel, by a German worker, Joseph Dietzgen.[13]

In this way, however, the revolutionary side of Hegelian philosophy was again taken up and at the same time freed from the idealist trimmings which with Hegel had prevented its consistent execution. The great basic thought that the world is not to be comprehended as a complex of ready-made *things*, but as a complex of processes, in which the things apparently stable no less than their mind images in our heads, the concepts, go through an uninterrupted change of coming into being and passing away, in which, in spite of all seeming accidentally and of all temporary retrogression, a progressive development asserts itself in the end–this great fundamental thought has, especially since the time of Hegel, so thoroughly permeated ordinary consciousness that in this generality it is now scarcely ever contradicted. But to acknowledge this fundamental thought in words and to apply it in reality in detail to each domain of investigation are two different things. If, however, in-

70

vestigation always proceeds from this standpoint, the demand for final solutions and eternal truths ceases once for all; one is always conscious of the necessary limitation of all acquired knowledge, of the fact that it is conditioned by the circumstances in which it was acquired. On the other hand, one no longer permits oneself to be imposed upon by the antithesis, insuperable for the still common old metaphysics, between true and false, good and bad, identical and different, necessary and accidental. One knows that these antitheses have only a relative validity; that that which is recognized now as true has also its latent false side which will later manifest itself, just as that which is now regarded as false has also its true side by virtue of which it could previously be regarded as true. One knows that what is maintained to be necessary is composed of sheer accidents and that the so-called accidental is the form behind which necessity hides itself and so on.

The old method of investigation and thought which Hegel calls "metaphysical," which preferred to investigate things as given, as fixed and stable, a method the relics of which still strongly haunt people's minds, had a great deal of historical justification in its day. It was necessary first to examine things before it was possible to examine processes. One had first to know what a particular thing was before one could observe the changes it was undergoing. And such was the case with natural science. The old metaphysics, which accepted things as finished objects, arose from a natural science which investigated dead and living things as finished objects. But when this investigation had progressed so far that it became possible to take the decisive step forward, that is, to pass on the systematic investigation of the changes which these things undergo in nature itself, then the last hour of the old metaphysic struck in the realm of philosophy also. And in fact, while natural science up

71

to the end of the last century was predominantly a collecting science, a science of finished things, in our century it is essentially a systematizing science, a science of the processes, of the origin and development of these things and of the interconnection which binds all these natural processes into one great whole. Physiology, which investigates the processes occurring in plant and animal organisms; embryology, which deals with the development of individual organisms from germs to maturity; geology, which investigates the gradual formation of the Earth's surface–all these are the offspring of our century.

But, above all, there are three great discoveries which have enabled our knowledge of the interconnection of natural processes to advance by leaps and bounds.

First, the discovery of the cell as the unit from whose multiplication and differentiation the whole plant and animal body develops. Not only is the development and growth of all higher organisms recognized to proceed according to a single general law, but the capacity of the cell to change indicates the way by which organisms can change their species and thus go through a more than individual development.

Second, the transformation of energy, which has demonstrated to us that all the so-called forces operative in the first instance in inorganic nature–mechanical force and its complement, so-called potential energy, heat, radiation (light, or radiant heat), electricity, magnetism, and chemical energy–are different forms of manifestation of universal motion, which pass into one another in definite proportions so that in place of a certain quantity of the one which disappears, a certain quantity of another makes its appearance and thus the whole motion of nature is reduced to this incessant process of transformation from one form into another.

Finally, the proof which Darwin first developed in connected form that the stock of organic products of nature environing us today, including man, is the result of a long process of evolution from a few originally unicellular germs, and that these again have arisen from protoplasm or albumen, which came into existence by chemical means.

Thanks to these three great discoveries, and the other immense advances in natural science, we have now arrived at the point where we can demonstrate the interconnection between the processes in nature not only in particular spheres but also the interconnection of these particular spheres on the whole, and so we can present in an approximately systematic form a comprehensive view of the interconnection in nature by means of the facts provided by an empirical science itself. To furnish this comprehensive view was formerly the task of so-called natural philosophy. It could do this only by putting in place of the real but as yet unknown interconnections–ideal, fancied ones,–filling in the missing facts by figments of the mind and bridging the actual gaps merely in imagination. In the course of this procedure it conceived many brilliant ideas and foreshadowed many later discoveries, but it also produced a considerable amount of nonsense, which indeed could not have been otherwise. Today, when one needs to comprehend the results of natural scientific investigation only dialectically, that is, in the sense of their own interconnection, in order to arrive at a "system of nature" sufficient for our time; when the dialectical character of this interconnection is forcing itself against their will even into the metaphysically-trained minds of the natural scientists, today natural philosophy is finally disposed of. Every attempt at resurrecting it would be not only superfluous but a step backwards.

But what is true of nature, which is hereby recognized also as a historical process of development, is likewise true of the history of society in all its branches and of the totality of all sciences which occupy themselves with things human (and divine). Here, too, the philosophy of history, of right, of religion, etc., has consisted in the substitution of an interconnection fabricated in the mind of the philosopher for the real interconnection to be demonstrated in the events; has consisted in the comprehension of history as a whole as well as in its separate parts, as the gradual realization of ideas—and naturally always only the pet ideas of the philosopher himself. According to this, history worked unconsciously but of necessity towards a certain ideal goal set in advance—as, for example, in Hegel, towards the realization of his Absolute Idea—and the unalterable trend towards this Absolute Idea formed the inner interconnection in the events of history. A new mysterious providence—unconscious or gradually coming into consciousness—was thus put in the place of the real, still unknown interconnection. Here, therefore, just as in the realm of nature, it was necessary to do away with these fabricated, artificial interconnections by the discovery of the real ones—a task which ultimately amounts to the discovery of the general laws of motion which assert themselves as the ruling ones in the history of human society.

In one point, however, the history of the development of society proves to be essentially different from that of nature. In nature—in so far as we ignore man's reaction upon nature—there are only blind, unconscious agencies acting upon one another, out of whose interplay the general law comes into operation. Nothing of all that happens—whether in the innumerable apparent accidents observable upon the surface, or in the ultimate results which confirm the regularity inherent in these accidents—happens as a consciously desired aim. In the history of society, on the contrary, the actors are all endowed with consciousness, are men acting with deliberation or passion, working towards definite goals; nothing happens without a conscious purpose, without an intended aim. But this distinction, important as it is for historical investigation, particularly of single epochs and events, cannot alter the fact that the course of history is governed by inner general laws. For here, also, on the whole, in spite of the consciously desired aims of all individuals, accident apparently reigns on the surface. That which is willed happens but rarely; in the majority of instances the numerous desired ends cross and conflict with one another, or these ends themselves are from the outset incapable of realization, or the means of attaining them are insufficient. thus the conflicts of innumerable individual wills and individual actions in the domain of history produce a state of affairs entirely analogous to that prevailing in the realm of unconscious nature. The ends of the actions are intended, but the results which actually follow from these actions are not intended; or when they do seem to correspond to the end intended, they ultimately have consequences quite other than those intended. Historical events thus appear on the whole to be likewise governed by chance. But where on the surface accident holds sway, there actually it is always governed by inner, hidden laws, and it is only a matter of discovering these laws.

Men make their own history, whatever its outcome may be, in that each person follows his own consciously desired end, and it is precisely the resultant of these many wills operating in different directions, and of their manifold effects upon the outer world, that constitutes history. Thus it is also a question of what the many individuals desire. The will is determined by passion or deliberation. But the levers which immediately determine passion or deliberation are of very different kinds. Partly they may be external objects, partly ideal motives, ambition, "enthusiasm for truth and justice," personal hatred, or even purely individual whims of all kinds. But, on the one hand, we have seen that the many individual wills active in history for the most part produce results quite other than those intended–often quite the opposite; that their motives, therefore, in relation to the total result are likewise of only secondary importance. On the other hand, the further question arises: What driving forces in turn stand behind these motives? What are the historical forces which transform themselves into these motives in the brains of the actors?

The old materialism never put this question to itself. Its conception of history, in so far as it has one at all, is therefore essentially pragmatic; it divides men who act in history into noble and ignoble and then finds that as a rule the noble are defrauded and the ignoble are victorious. hence, it follows for the old materialism that nothing very edifying is to be gotten from the study of history, and for us that in the realm of history the old materialism becomes untrue to itself because it takes the ideal driving forces which operate there as ultimate causes, instead of investigating what is behind them, what are the driving forces of these driving forces. This inconsistency does not lie in the fact that ideal driving forces are recognized, but in the investigation not being carried further back behind these into their motive causes. On the other hand, the philosophy of history, particularly as represented by Hegel, recognizes that the ostensible and also the really operating motives of men who act in history are by no means the ultimate causes of historical events; that behind these motives are other motive powers, which have to be discovered. But it does not seek these powers in history itself, it imports them rather from outside, from philosophical ideology, into history. Hegel, for example, instead of explaining the history of ancient Greece out of its own inner interconnections, simply maintains that it is nothing more than the working out of "forms of beautiful individuality," the realization of a "work of art"as such. He says much in this connection about the old Greeks that is fine and profound, but that does not prevent us today from refusing to be put off with such an explanation, which is a mere manner of speech.

When, therefore, it is a question of investigating the driving powers which–consciously or unconsciously, and indeed very often unconsciously–lie behind the motives of men who act in history and which constitute the real ultimate driving forces of history, then it is not a question so much of the motives of single individuals, however eminent, as of those motives which set in motion great masses, whole people, and again whole classes of the people in each people; and this, too, not merely for an instant, like the transient flaring up of a straw-fire which quickly dies down, but as a lasting action resulting in a great historical transformation. To ascertain the driving causes which here in the minds of acting masses and their leaders–to so-called great men–are reflected as conscious motives, clearly or unclearly, directly or in an ideological, even glorified, form–is the only path which can put us on the track of the laws holding sway both in history as a whole, and at particular periods and in particular lands. Everything which sets men in motion must go through their minds; but what form it will take in the mind will depend very much upon the circumstances. The workers have by no means become reconciled to capitalist machine industry, even though they no longer simply break the machines to pieces, as they still did in 1848 on the Rhine River.

But while in all earlier periods the investigation of these driving causes of history was almost impossible–on account of the complicated and concealed interconnections between them and their effects—our present period has so far simplified these interconnections that the riddle could be solved. Since the establishment of large-scale industry—that is, at least since the European peace of 1815—it has been no longer a secret to any man in England that the whole political struggle there pivoted on the claims to supremacy of two classes: the landed aristocracy and the bourgeoisie (middle class). In France, with the return of the Bourbons, the same fact was perceived, the historians of the Restoration period, from Augustin Thierry to François Guizot, François Mignet, and Adolphe Thiers, speak of it everywhere as the key to the understanding of all French history since the Middle Ages. And since 1830, the working class, the proletariat, has been recognized in both countries as a third competitor for power. Conditions had become so simplified that one would have had to close one's eyes deliberately not to see in the light of these three great classes and in the conflict of their interests the driving force of modern history—at least in the two most advanced countries.

But how did these classes come into existence? If it was possible at first glance still to ascribe the origin of the great, formerly feudal landed property—at least in the first instance—to political causes, to taking possession by force, this could not be done in regard to the bourgeoise and the proletariat. Here, the origin and development of two great classes was seen to lie clearly and palpably in purely economic causes. And it was just as clear that in the struggle between landed property and the bourgeoisie, no less than in the struggle between the bourgeoisie and the proletariat, it was a question, first and foremost, of economic interests, to the furtherance of which political power was intended to serve merely as a means. Bourgeoisie and proletariat both arose in consequences of a transformation of the economic conditions, more precisely, of the mode of production. The transition, first from guild handicrafts to manufacture, and then from manufacture to large-scale industry, with steam and mechanical power, had caused the development of these two classes. At a certain stage, the new productive forces set in motion by the bourgeoisie–in the first place the division of labor and the combination of many detail laborers in one general manufactory–and the conditions and requirements of exchange, developed through these productive forces, became incompatible with the existing order of production handed down by history and sanctified by law–that is to say, incompatible with the privileges of the guild and the numerous other personal and local privileges (which were only so many fetters to the unprivileged estates) of the feudal order to society. The productive forces represented by the bourgeoisie rebelled against the order of production represented by the feudal landlords and the guild-masters. The result is known, the feudal fetters were smashed, gradually in England, at one blow in France. In Germany, the process is not yet finished. But just as, at a definite stage of its development, manufacture came into conflict with the feudal order of production, so now large-scale industry has already come into conflict with the bourgeois order or production established in its place. Tied down by this order, by the narrow limits of the capitalist mode of production, this industry produces, on the one hand, an ever increasingly proletarianization of the great mass of the people, and on the other hand, an ever greater mass of unsalable products. Overproduction and mass misery, each the cause of the other–that is the absurd contradiction which is its outcome, and which of necessity calls for the liberation of the productive forces by means of a change in the mode of production.

In modern history at least it is, therefore, proved that all political struggles are class struggles, and all class struggles for emancipation, despite their necessarily political form–for every class struggle is a political struggle–turn ultimately on the question of economic emancipation. Therefore, here at least, the state–the political order–is the subordination, and civil society–the realm of economic relations–the decisive element. The traditional conception, to which Hegel, too, pays homage, saw in the state the determining element, and in civil society the element determined by it. Appearances correspond to this. As all the driving forces of the actions of any individual person must pass through his brain, and transform themselves into motives of his will in order to set him into action, so also all the needs of civil society–no matter which class happens to be the ruling one–must pass through the will of the state in order to secure general validity in the form of laws. That is the formal aspect of the matter–the one which is self-evident. The question arises, however, what is the content of this merely formal will–of the individual as well as of the state–and whence is this content derived? Why is just this willed and not something else? If we enquire into this, we discover that in modern history the will of the state is, on the whole, determined by the changing needs of civil society, but the supremacy of this or that class, in the last resort, by the development of the productive forces and relations of exchange.

But if even in our modern era, with its gigantic means of production and communication, the state is not an independent domain with an independent development, but one whose existence as well as development is to be explained in the last resort by the economic conditions of life of society, then this must be still more true of all earlier times when the production of the material life of man was not yet carried on with these abundant auxiliary means, and when, therefore, the necessity of such production must have exercised a still greater mastery over men. If the state even today, in the era of big industry and of railways, is on the whole only a reflection, in concentrated form, of the economic needs of the class controlling production, then this must have been much more so in an epoch when each generation of men was forced to spend a far greater part of its aggregate lifetime in satisfying material needs, and was therefore much more dependent on them than we are today. An examination of the history of earlier periods, as soon as it is seriously undertaken from this angle, most abundantly confirms this. But, of course, this cannot be gone into here.

If the state and public law are determined by economic relations, so, too, of course, is private law, which indeed in essence only sanctions the existing economic relations between individuals which are normal in the given circumstances. The form in which this happens can, however, vary considerably. It is possible, as happened in England, in harmony with the whole national development, to retain in the main the forms of the old feudal laws while giving them a bourgeois content; in fact, directly reading a bourgeois meaning into the feudal name. But, also, as happened in Western continental Europe, roman law, the first world law of a commodity-producing society, with its unsurpassably fine elaboration of all the essential legal relations of simple commodity owners (of buyers and sellers, debtors and creditors, contracts, obligations, etc.) can be taken as the foundation. In which case, for the benefit of a still petty-bourgeois and semi-feudal society, it can either be reduced to the level of such a society simply through judicial practice (common law) or, with the help of allegedly enlightened, moralizing jurists it can be worked into a special code of law to correspond with such social level–a code which in these circumstances will be a bad one also from the legal standpoint [for instance, Prussian Landrecht (law of the land)]. But after a great bourgeois revolution it is, however, also possible for such a classic law code of bourgeois society as the French *Code Civile* to be worked out upon the basis of this same Roman Law. If, therefore, bourgeois legal rules merely express the economic life conditions of society in legal form, then they can do so well or ill according to circumstances.

The state presents itself to us as the first ideological power over man. Society creates for itself an organ for the safeguarding of its common interests against internal and external attacks. This organ is the state power. Hardly come into being, this organ makes itself independent *vis-a-vis* society; and, indeed, the more so, the more it becomes the organ of a particular class, the more it directly enforces the supremacy of that class. The fight of the oppressed class against the ruling class becomes necessarily a political fight, a fight first of all against the political dominance of this class. The consciousness of the interconnection between this political struggle and its economic basis becomes dulled and can be lost altogether. While this is not wholly the case with the participants, it almost always happens with the historians. Of the ancient sources on the struggles within the Roman Republic, only Appian[14] tells us clearly and distinctly what was at issue in the last resort—namely, landed property.

But once the state has become an independent power *vis-a-vis* society, it produces forthwith a further ideology. It is indeed among professional politicians, theorists of public law, and jurists of private law, that the connection with economic facts gets lost. Since in each particular case, the economic facts must assume the form of juristic motives in order to receive legal sanction; and since, in so doing, consideration of course has to be given to the whole legal system already in operation, the juristic form is, in consequence, made everything and the economic content nothing. Public law and private law are treated as independent spheres, each being capable of and needing a systematic presentation by the consistent elimination of all inner contradictions.

Still higher ideologies, that is, such as are still further removed from the material, economic basis, take the form of philosophy and religion. Here the interconnection between conceptions and their material conditions of existence becomes more and more complicated, more and more obscured by intermediate links. But the interconnection exists. Just as the whole Renaissance period, from the middle of the 15th century, was an essential product of the towns and, therefore, of the burghers,[15] so also was the subsequently newly-awakened philosophy. Its content was in essence only the philosophical expression of the thoughts corresponding to the development of the small and middle burghers into a big bourgeoisie. Among last century's Englishmen and Frenchmen who in many cases were just as much political economists as philosophers, this is clearly evident; and we have proved it above in regard to the Hegelian school.

We will now, in addition, deal only briefly with religion, since the latter stands further away from material life and seems to be most alien to it. Religion arose in very primitive times from erroneous, primitive conceptions of men about their own nature and external nature surrounding them. Every ideology, however, once it has arisen, develops in connection with the given concept-material, and develops this material further; otherwise, it would not be an ideology, that is, occupation with thoughts as with independent entities, developing independently and subject only to their own laws. In the last analysis, the material life conditions of the persons inside whose heads this thought process goes on determine the course of the process, which of necessity remains unknown to these persons, for otherwise there would be an end to all ideology. These original religious notions, therefore, which in the main are common to each group of kindred peoples, develop, after the group separates, in a manner peculiar to each people, according to the conditions of life falling to their lot. For a number of groups of peoples, and particularly for the Aryans (so-called Indo-Europeans) this process has been shown in detail by comparative mythology. The gods thus fashioned within each people were national gods, whose domain extended no farther than the national territory which they were to protect; on the other side of its boundaries, other gods held undisputed sway. They could continue to exist, in imagination, only as long as the nation existed; they fell with its fall. The Roman world empire, the economic conditions of whose origin we do not need to examine here, brought about this downfall of the old nationalities. The old national gods decayed, even those of the Romans, which also were patterned to suit only the narrow confines of the city of Rome. The need to complement the world empire by means of a world religion was clearly revealed in the attempts made to recognize all foreign gods that were the least bit respectable and provide altars for them in Rome alongside the native gods. But a new world religion is not to be made in this fashion, by imperial decree. The new world religion, Christianity, had already quietly come into being, out of a mixture of generalized Oriental, particularly Jewish, theology, and vulgarized Greek, particularly Stoic, philosophy. What it originally looked like has to be first laboriously discovered, since its official form, as it has been handed down to us, is merely that in which it became the state religion to which purpose it was adapted by the

Council of Nicaea. The fact that already after 250 years it became the state religion suffices to show that it was the religion in correspondence with the conditions of the time. In the Middle Ages, in the same measure as feudalism developed, Christianity grew into the religious counterpart to it, with a corresponding feudal hierarchy. And when the burghers began to thrive, there developed, in opposition to feudal Catholicism, the Protestant heresy, which first appeared in Southern France among the Albigenses,[16] at the time the cities there reached the highest point of their florescence. The Middle Ages had attached to theology all the other forms of ideology–philosophy, politics, jurisprudence–and made them subdivision of theology. It thereby constrained every social and political movement to take on a theological form. The sentiments of the masses were fed with religion to the exclusion of all else; it was therefore necessary to put forward their own interests in a religious guise in order to produce a great tempest. And just as the burghers from the beginning brought into being an appendage of propertyless urban plebeians, day laborers and servants of all kinds, belonging to no recognized social estate, precursors of the later proletariat, so likewise heresy soon became divided into a burgher-moderate heresy and a plebeian-revolutionary one, the latter an abomination to the burgher heretics themselves.

The ineradicability of the Protestant heresy corresponded to the invincibility of the rising burghers. When these burghers had become sufficiently strengthened, their struggle against the feudal nobility, which till then had been predominantly local, began to assume national dimensions. The first great action occurred in Germany–the so-called Reformation. The burghers were neither powerful enough nor sufficiently developed to be able to unite under their banner the remaining rebellious estates–the plebeians of the towns, the lower nobility, and the peasants on the land. At first, the nobles were defeated; the peasants rose in a revolt which formed the peak of the whole revolutionary struggle; the cities left them in the lurch, and thus the revolution succumbed to the armies of the secular princes who reaped the whole profit. Thenceforward, Germany disappears for three centuries from the ranks of countries playing an independent active part in history. But, beside the German Catholic Priest, Luther appeared the Frenchman Theologian, Calvin. With true French acuity, he put the bourgeois character of the Reformation in the forefront, republicanized and democratized the Church. While the Lutheran Reformation in Germany degenerated and reduced the country to rack and ruin, the Calvinist Reformation served as a banner for the republicans in Geneva, in Holland, and in Scotland, freed Holland from Spain and from the German Empire, and provided the ideological costume for the second act of the bourgeois revolution, which was taking place in England. Here, Calvinism justified itself as the true religious disguise of the interests of the bourgeoisie of that time, and on this account did not attain full recognition when the revolution ended in 1689 in a compromise between one part of the nobility and the bourgeoisie. The English state Church was reestablished; but not in its earlier form of a Catholicism which had the king for its pope, being, instead, strongly Calvinized. The old state Church had celebrated the merry Catholic Sunday and had fought against the dull Calvinist one. The new, bourgeoisified Church introduced the latter, which adorns England to this day.

In France, the Calvinist minority was suppressed in 1685 and either Catholized or driven out of the country. But what was the good? Already at that time the freethinker Pierre Bayle was at the height of his activity, and in 1694 Voltaire was born. The forcible measures of Louis XIV only made it easier for the

French bourgeoisie to carry through its revolution in the irreligious, exclusively political form which alone was suited to a developed bourgeoisie. Instead of Protestants, freethinkers took their seats in the national assemblies. Thereby Christianity entered into its final stage. It was incapable of doing any future service to any progressive class as the ideological garb of its aspirations. It became more and more the exclusive possession of the ruling classes; they apply it as a mere means of government, to keep the lower classes within bounds. Moreover, each of the different classes uses its own appropriate religion: the landed nobility–Catholic Jesuitism, or Protestant orthodoxy; the liberal and radical bourgeoisie–rationalism; and it makes little difference whether these gentlemen themselves believe in their respective religions or not.

We see, therefore: religion, once formed, always contains traditional material, just as in all ideological domains tradition forms a great conservative force. But the transformations which this material undergoes spring from class relations–that is to say, out of the economic relations of the people who execute these transformations. And here that is sufficient.

In the above, it could only be a question of giving a general sketch of the Marxist conception of history, at most with a few illustrations, as well. The proof must be derived from history itself; and, in this regard, it may be permitted to say that is has been sufficiently furnished in other writings. This conception, however, puts an end to philosophy in the realm of history, just as the dialectical conception of nature makes all natural philosophy both unnecessary and impossible. It is no longer a question anywhere of inventing interconnections from out of our brains, but of discovering them in the facts. For philosophy, which has been expelled from nature and history, there remains only the realm of pure thought, so far as it is left: the theory of the laws of the thought process itself, logic and dialectics.

With the Revolution of 1848, "educated" Germany said farewell to theory and went over to the field of practice. Small production and manufacture, based upon manual labor, were superseded by real large-scale industry. Germany again appeared on the world market. The new little German Empire abolished at least the most crying of the abuses with which this development had been obstructed by the system of petty states, the relics of feudalism, and bureaucratic management. But to the same degree that speculation abandoned the philosopher's study in order to set up its temple in the Stock Exchange. Educated Germany lost the great aptitude for theory which had been the glory of Germany in the days of its deepest political humiliation–the aptitude for purely scientific investigation, irrespective of whether the result obtained was practically applicable or not, whether likely to offend the police authorities or not. Official German natural science, it is true, maintained its position in the front rank, particularly in the field of specialized research. But even the American journal *Science* rightly remarks that the decisive advances in the sphere of the comprehensive correlation of particular facts and their generalization into laws are now being made much more in England, instead of, as formerly, in Germany. And in the sphere of the historical sciences, philosophy included, the old fearless zeal for theory has now disappeared completely, along with classical philosophy. Inane eclecticism and an anxious concern for career and income, descending to the most vulgar job-hunting, occupy its place. The official representatives of these sciences have become the undisguised ideologists of the bourgeoisie and the existing state–but at a time when both stand in open antagonism to the working class.

Only among the working class does the German aptitude for theory remain unimpaired. Here, it cannot be exterminated. Here, there is no concern for careers, for profit-making, or for gracious patronage from above. On the contrary, the more ruthlessly and disinterestedly science proceeds the more it finds itself in harmony with the interest and aspirations of the workers. The new tendency, which recognized that the key to the understanding of the whole history of society lies in the history of the development of labor, from the outset addressed itself by preference to the working class and here found the response which it neither sought nor expected from officially recognized science. The German working-class movement is the inheritor of German classical philosophy.

Part Three

Engels at 200: Intellectual Giant and Rebel

by
Thomas Riggins

Friedrich[17] Engels, Karl Marx's life-long friend and co-developer of what has become known as Marxism, scientific socialism, dialectical materialism, and in the twentieth century as a result of the Russian Revolution, Marxism-Leninism, was born two hundred years ago on November 28, 1820, in what is now Wuppertal, Germany (then Barman, Prussia). This article commemorates the bicentenary of Engels's birth by pointing out some of his most important contributions to the development of Marxist theory.

Marx and Engels first met in 1842 in Cologne, Germany. Engels was 22 and had been active as a student in the democratic and progressive movements in Prussia and was on his way to England to join in the management of a factory partially owned by his father. His father, a conservative bourgeois businessman, had taken Engels out of his university studies because he disapproved of his involvement in radical student movements opposed to the undemocratic Prussian monarchy. These movements were based based on the philosophical and political works of G.W.F. Hegel (1770-1831), and the students were known as the "Young Hegelians." Marx was the editor of a radical democratic newspaper (*Rheinische Zeitung*), and Engels wanted to meet him. Engels had already made a name for himself as a radical journalist while a student. After Marx hired him as a foreign correspondent, he continued on to Manchester where the factory was located. His father's hope that he would settle down and become a respectable businessman was not going to be realized.

Engels spent two years in England, where he met with radical working-class leaders and wrote articles on current events and an important essay on political economy from a socialist point of view, as well as worked in his father's factory. In 1844, on a trip back to Prussia, he stopped off in Paris to visit with Marx; the two had corresponded and wanted to meet up to compare their views on socialism. Marx was in Paris as a refugee, as the authorities in Cologne had expelled him for his political views. They spent ten days together and found out they had the same world outlook. They decided to collaborate and produce a joint work which put forth their views on socialism and philosophical materialism supporting the working class, as opposed to the Young Hegelians who based their views on philosophical idealism and were liberals opposed to communist and socialist views.

Engels continued on to Prussia. A year later, their collaboration resulted in the publication of the first of many works the two would produce in the creation of dialectical materialism— the philosophy of the working-class struggle for emancipation and the creation of socialism. *The Holy Family; or Critique of Critical Criticism: Against Bruno Bauer and Company* was not a full-fledged exposition of dialectical materialism, but it was a harbinger of things to come.

Engels stayed in Prussia from the fall of 1844 to the spring of 1845. While there he wrote his well-known *The Condition of the Working Class in England*. The book created quite a stir in Germany when it was published in 1845. Engels discussed the working-class movement in terms of materialism and the need for socialism. He also stressed the importance of workers' organizations and especially unions and the use of strikes to win acceptance of their demands from the bourgeoisie. He was also active in the socialist movement, wrote articles for the socialist press, and, as might have been expected, became estranged from his conservative father.

Things were getting too hot in Prussia for Engels. With the authorities upset with his activities and the police spying on him, Engels worried about being arrested, so in the spring of 1845 he moved to Brussels. He chose Brussels because Marx was there, as he had to leave Paris for the same reasons. It was at this time that the pair worked out a full-fledged version of dialectical materialism. Engels had almost gotten there on his own, but Marx had worked out a more advanced view that Engels immediately recognized as such. Here they decided to collaborate on another book to iron out their ideas and solidify their new philosophy in contradistinction to both the objective idealism of Hegel and the materialism of Feuerbach (an influential student of Hegel whose materialist system inspired Marx and Engels but who was not dialectical in his thinking).

Their new book *The German Ideology* was finished by 1846 but never published in their lifetime. It had been accepted for publication, but political and financial difficulties had arisen, and the publication was shelved until after the Russian Revolution when it was published by the Soviets. It had served its purpose though; in writing it Marx and Engels had finally arrived at full agreement both politically and philosophically and were ready to devote their lives to the struggle for communism. They packed away the manuscript and, as Marx remarked, "left it to the gnawing criticism of the mice."

Marx and Engels became involved in building socialist organizations in Brussels, and their writings were being spread in Germany and elsewhere through the socialist press. There were many different versions of "socialism" in the 1840s, but dialectical materialism began to slowly catch on to such an extent that in 1846 the Brussels followers of Marx and Engels sent Engels to Paris to make contact with the leading French groups and German exiles advocating socialism and democratic rights. So impressed were the leading French socialists that the editor of a major socialist paper, *La Réforme*, appointed Engels as a correspondent. He also made contact with the leading group of German socialist exiles in Paris, The League of the Just.

In 1847 the League asked Marx and Engels to become members. The influence exerted by their ideas soon came to dominate the thinking of most League members, and in June Engels went to London to attend the League's First Congress. By the end of the congress the League had renamed itself the Communist League, and a new slogan, "Workers of the World, Unite," was adopted, superseding the bourgeois liberal (and male chauvinist, pace Schiller and Beethoven) "All Men Are Brothers." Brussels became the center for the Communist League and its internationally circulated newspaper *Deutsche Brüsseler Zeitung*, with Marx and Engels writing the articles on theory.

In the fall of 1847 Engels went to Paris to help the Communist League and prepare for its second congress. He reworked the draft program the league had drawn up, named it the "Manifesto of the Communist Party," and sent it to Marx to look over. The second congress (December 1847) adopted dialectical materialism as its policy, and Marx and Engels collaborated on getting the manifesto ready for the press. It was published in February 1848, and the international communist movement was launched.

The publication coincided with the 1848 February Revolution in France. Revolutions broke out all over Europe that year as the revolutionary bourgeoisie consolidated its political and economic power at the expense of the remnants of the old feudalist order. In France, Louis Philippe, the last of the French kings, was forced to abdicate, and the Second Republic was proclaimed. The revolution spread to Germany and southern and eastern Europe. Engels joined Marx in Cologne to work at the *Neue Rheinische Zeitung*, the German daily newspaper published by Marx.

In 1849 Engels participated in revolutionary fighting in the Rhine Province, and when the revolutionaries were defeated, he escaped to Switzerland. From there he made his way to London and helped reorganize the Communist League. In 1850 he wrote another of his important historical works, *The Peasant War in Germany*.

The year 1850 also saw Engels's return to Manchester and his father's factory. Marx was now living in London, and the two were in constant communication. With the revolution having been defeated, they now engaged in research and the elaboration of their theories. Because Engels was running his father's factory, he was able to help Marx financially; this allowed Marx the time he needed to write *Das Kapital* (published in 1867), one of two most important books of the 19th century (the other being Darwin's *Origin of Species*, published in 1859). Lenin said that without Engels's aid Marx would have been "unable to complete" *Das Kapital*. As it was, Marx only lived to complete volume I, and Engels, with Marx's drafts and notes, completed volumes II and III and saw them through to print.

Throughout the 1850s Marx, and especially Engels, concentrated on elaborating the practical aspects of dialectical materialism regarding the struggles of the working class to create unions and in the various national liberation movements that existed at that time, such as in Ireland, Poland, Hungary, the Balkans, and India, including the anti-slavery movement in the U.S.

In 1864 Marx and Engels were instrumental in the founding of the First International. Throughout its existence Engels was a major contributor to the International's positions on war, colonization, the U.S. Civil War, and the fight against the anarchist movements, which opposed the views of Marx and Engels and the Communist League, under the influence of Mikhail Bakunin (whose views are kept alive and well in the 21st century by anarchists representing the views of the petty bourgeois radicals and not the working class).

In 1872 or 1873 Engels began another important book, *Dialectics of Nature*, which he worked on intermittently for ten years but never finished. After Engels's death Edward Bernstein showed the manuscript to Albert Einstein, who thought it worth publishing even though the physics and mathematical parts were weak and out of date. It was published, finally, by the Soviet Union in 1925 (the Marx-Engels Institute). It has limited value, since the sciences have made qualitatively giant strides from the mid-19th century, but it shows how Engels used dialectical materialism to interpret scientific advances dialectically. It also has many interesting sections in which Engels put forth the rudiments of ideas that were later to become part of our contemporary scientific understanding of the world (especially in his discussion of human evolution and some aspects of modern physics, although in antiquated terms no longer in use).

One of the reasons his book on nature was never completed was that he was busy on other important projects in the 1870s, such as following the developments and advising the growing socialist parties in France, Germany, England, and other countries while also writing important theoretical works: *The Housing Question, On Authority, and The Bakuninists at*

Work (all in 1873), as well as one of the most important works in all Marxist literature, *Anti-Dühring* (1878).

Anti-Dühring covered the whole gamut of dialectical materialism, and three chapters on the history of socialism were so popular that Engels was asked to issue them as a separate work. He reworked these chapters and in 1880 published them in the work we know as *Socialism: Utopian and Scientific.*

The great collaboration of Marx and Engels came to an end on March 14, 1883, when Marx died at age 65, leaving Engels alone as the *de facto* intellectual leader of the world socialist movement. Marx left behind a trove of unfinished works which was left for Engels to edit and see published. Engels had, as well, two more major works of his own to complete in the eleven years left to him.

Engels managed to get volume 2 of *Das Kapital* properly arranged and edited, and it was published in 1885, followed by volume 3 in 1894. He put so much work into these volumes that Lenin said they should be seen as joint works of Marx and Engels. At the same time he was editing Marx's manuscripts and turning pages of notes and hastily jotted down ideas into readable texts, he managed to write two works of his own that have become Marxist classics. In 1884 *The Origin of the Family, Private Property, and the State* came out ("one of the fundamental works of modern socialism" -Lenin). His final major work, *Ludwig Feuerbach and the Outcome of Classical German Philosophy*, was published in 1886.

It was in this period that Engels advised the Marxist parties to avoid sectarianism and dogma and to work to develop mass working-class parties. He also gave the classical definition of "opportunism" (still a big problem)–"letting the great basic considerations be consigned to oblivion by transient daily interests," in other words, "sacrificing the future of the movement to the present."

This period also saw the founding of the Second International (1889) in Paris in which Engels played a leading role. The First International (International Workingmen's Association) had been basically set up by Marx and Engels in 1864 and was dissolved in 1876 to prevent its being taken over by the anarchist followers of Bakunin (who died that year in Bern, Switzerland). This international, which excluded the anarchists, lasted to 1916 when it fell apart because most of its national units, pledged to resist war, ended up supporting their own nations in World War I. It was succeeded by the Third International (1919–1943).

Engels, who in these years maintained his position as the most influential leader of the world socialist movement, began to have health problems in the 1890s and died of laryngeal cancer on August 5, 1895. A short time before his death, a young Russian revolutionary, V. I. Ulyanov (Lenin), made a trip to London, hoping to meet with Engels but was turned away because Engels was too ill to meet with anyone. After his death his daughter Eleanor Aveling and two close friends, Friedrich Lessner and Eduard Bernstein, carried out his last request to be cremated and his ashes scattered in the ocean off Beachy Head, near Eastbourne in East Sussex on the south coast of England.

Friedrich Engels and Early Christianity

by
Thomas Riggins

Part 1

This[18] is the season to remind all our Christian friends of the relationship between Christianity and Marxism-Leninism and the working class movement. Engels ("On the History of Early Christianity") tells us that there are "notable points of resemblance" between the early working class movement and Christianity.

First, both movements were made up of oppressed poor people from the lower ranks of society. Christianity was a religion of slaves and people without rights subjugated by the state and very similar to the types of poor oppressed working people that founded the earliest socialist and worker's organizations in modern times.

Second, both movements held out the hope of salvation and liberation from tyranny and oppression: one in the world to come, the other in this world.

Third, both movements were (and in some places still are) attacked by the powers that be and were discriminated against, their members killed or imprisoned, despised, and treated as enemies of the status quo.

Fourth, despite fierce persecution both movements grew and became more powerful. After three hundred years of struggle Christians took control of the Roman Empire and became a world religion. The worker's movement is still struggling. After its first modern revolutionary appearance as a fully self-conscious movement (1848) it achieved a major impetus in the later part of the nineteenth century with the growth of the First and Second Internationals, and the German Social Democratic movement. It too is now a worldwide movement with Socialist, Social Democratic and Communist parties spread around the world. [The rise and fall of the USSR was a bump in the road the consequences of which have yet to be determined.]

The Book of Acts reveals that the early Christians were primitive communists sharing their goods in common and leading a collective lifestyle. This original form of Christianity was wiped out when the Roman Empire under Constantine imposed Christianity as the official religion of the state and set up the Catholic Church in order to make sure that the religious teachings of Jesus and the early followers of his movement would be perverted to protect the interests of the wealthy and the power of the state.

With few exceptions, all forms of modern day Christianity are descended from this faux version, based on a mixture of Jewish religious elements and the practices of Greco-Roman paganism, and only the modern working class and progressive movements (basically secular) carry on in the spirit of egalitarianism and socialism of the founder of Christianity.

Engels points out that there were many attempts in history (especially from the Middle Ages up to modern times) to reestablish the original communistic Christianity of Jesus and his early followers.

These attempts manifested themselves as peasant uprisings through the middle ages which tried to overthrow feudal oppression and create a world based on the teaching of Jesus and his Apostles.

These movements failed giving rise to the state sanctioned Christianity of modern times. Engels mentions some of these movements–i.e., the Bohemian Taborites led by Jan Zizka ("of glorious memory") and the German Peasant War. These movements are now represented, Engels points out, by the working men communists since the 1830s.

Engels reveals that misleadership is also a problem in these early movements (and still is today I would add) due to the low levels of education found amongst the poor and oppressed. He quotes a contemporary witness, Lucian of Samosata ("the Voltaire of classic antiquity"). Engels says, the Christians "despise all material goods without distinction and own them in common–doctrines which they have accepted in good faith, without demonstration or proof. And when a skillful impostor who knows how to make clever use of circumstances comes to them, he can manage to get rich in a short time and laugh up his sleeve over these simpletons." The Pat Robertsons and Jerry Falwell types have been around for a long time. I am sure readers can add a long list of names.

Part 2

Engels views on early Christianity were formed from his reading of what he considered "the only scientific basis" for such study, namely the new critical works by German scholars of religion.

First were the works of the *Tubingen School*, including David Strauss (*The Life of Jesus*). This school has shown that:

1. The Gospels are late writings based on now lost original sources from the time of Jesus and his followers
2. Only four of Paul's letters are by him
3. All miracles must be left out of account if you want a scientific view
4. All contradictory presentations of the same events must also be rejected.

This school then wants to preserve what it can of the history of early Christianity. By the way, this is essentially what Thomas Jefferson tried to do when he made his own version of the New Testament.

A second school was based on the writings of *Bruno Bauer*. What Bauer did was to show that Christianity would have remained a Jewish sect if it had not, in the years after the death of its founder, mutated by contact with Greco-Roman paganism, into a new religion capable of becoming a world-wide force. Bauer showed that Christianity, as we know it, did not come into the Roman world from the outside ("from

Judea") but that it was "that world's own product." Christianity owes as much to Zeus as to Yahweh.

Engels maintains that *The Book of Revelation* is the only book in the New Testament that can be properly dated by means of its internal evidence. It can be dated to around 67-68 AD since the famous number 666, as the mark of the beast or the Antichrist, represents the name of the emperor Nero according to the rules of numerology. Nero was overthrown in 68 AD. This book (Revelation), Engels says, is the best source of the views of the early Christians since it is much earlier than any of the Gospels and may actually have been the work the apostle John (which the Gospel and letters bearing his name were not).

In this book we will not find any of the views that characterize official Christianity as we have it from the time of the emperor Constantine to the present day. It is purely a Jewish phenomenon in Revelation. There is no *trinity* as *God* has *seven spirits* (so the *Holy Ghost* is impossible Engels remarks). *Jesus Christ* is not *God* but his *son*, he is not even equal in status to his father. Nevertheless, he has pretty high status, his followers are called his "slaves" by John. Jesus, according to Engels, is, "an emanation of God, existing from all eternity but subordinate to God" just as the seven spirits are. Moses is more or less on an equal footing with Jesus in the eyes of God. There is no mention of the later belief in original sin. John still thought of himself as a Jew. There is no idea at this time of "Christianity" as a new religion.

In this period, there were many "end of time" revelations in circulation both in the Semitic and in the Greco-Roman world. They all proclaimed that God was (or the gods were) pissed off at humanity and had to be appeased by sacrifices. John's revelation was *unique* because it proclaimed, "by one great voluntary sacrifice of a mediator the sins of all times and all men were atoned for once and for all–in respect of the faithful."

Since all peoples and races could be saved this is what, according to Engels, "enabled Christianity to develop into a universal religion." [Just as the concept of the workers of the world uniting to break their chains and build a worldwide communist future makes Marxism-Leninism a universal philosophy.]

In Heaven before the throne of God are 144,000 Jews (12,000 from each tribe). In the second rank of the saved are the non-Jewish converts to John's sect. Engels points out that neither the "dogma nor the morals" of later Christianity are to be found in this earliest of Christian expressions.

Some Muslims would presumably not like this Heaven, not only are there no (female) virgins in it, but there are also no women whatsoever. In fact, the 144,000 Jews have never been "defiled" by contact with women! This is a men's only club.

Engels says that the book shows a spirit of "struggle," of having to fight against the entire world and a willingness to do so. He says the Christians of today lack that spirit but that it survives in the working class movement. We must remember he was writing this in 1894.

There were other sects of Christianity springing up at this time too. John's sect eventually died out and the Christianity that won out was an amalgam of different groups who finally came together around the Council of Nicaea (325 AD). Those who did not sign on were themselves persecuted out of existence by the new Christian state.

We can see the analogy to the early sects of socialists and communists, says Engels. We can also see what happened after the Russian Revolution (Leninists, Stalinists, Trotskyists, Bukharinites, Maoists, etc.). Here in the US today we have the

CPUSA, the SWP, Worker's World, Revolutionary CP, Socialist Party, Sparticists, and etc.).

Engels thought that sectarianism was a thing of the past in the socialist movement because the movement had matured and outgrown it. This, we now know, was a temporary state of affairs at the end of the 19th Century with the consolidation of the German SPD. The widespread sectarianism of today suggests the worker's movement is still in its infancy.

Engels says this sectarianism is due to the confusion and backwardness of the thinking of the masses and the preponderate role that leaders play due to this backwardness. The Russian masses of 1917 and the Chinese of 1949 were a far different base than the German working class of the 1890s.

"This confusion," Engels writes, "is to be seen in the formation of numerous sects which fight against each other with at least the same zeal as against the common external enemy [China vs USSR, Stalin and Trotsky, Stalin and Tito, Vietnam vs China border war, Albania vs China and USSR, ad nauseam]. So as it was with early Christianity, so it was in the beginning of the socialist movement [and still is, *pace* Engels!], no matter how much that worried the well meaning worthies [entitled people]who preached unity where no unity was possible."

Finally, for those fans of the 60s sexual revolution, Engels says that many of the sects of early Christianity took the opposite view of John and actually promoted sexual freedom and free love as part of the new dispensation. They lost out. Engels says this sexual liberation was also found in the early socialist movement. He would not, I think, have approved of the excessive prudery of the Soviets.

Part 3

> "Here is wisdom. Let him that hath understanding count the number of the beast: for it is the number of a man; and his number is six hundred threescore and six."
>
> Revelation 13:18

In the last part of his essay Engels explains that the purpose of the Book of Revelation (by John of Patmos) was to communicate its religious vision to the seven churches of Asia Minor and to the larger sect of Jewish Christians that they represented.

At this time, circa 69 AD, the entire Mediterranean world much of the of Near East and Western Europe were under the control of the Roman Empire. This was a multicultural empire made of hundreds of tribes, groups, cities and peoples. Within the empire was a vast underclass of workers, freedmen, slaves and peasants whose exploited labor was lived off of by a ruling class of landed aristocrats and merchants. In 69 AD the empire was in essence a military dictatorship controlled by the army and led by the emperor (from the Latin word for "general"–imperator).

At this time there were peoples but no nations in our sense of the word. "Nations became possible," Engels says, "only through the downfall of Roman world domination." The effects of which are still being felt in the Middle East and parts of Europe, especially eastern Europe.

112

For the exploited masses of the Empire, it was basically impossible to resist the military power of Rome. There were uprisings and slave revolts, but they were always put down by the legions. This was the background for what became a great revolutionary movement of the poor and the exploited, a movement that became Christianity.

The purpose of the movement was to escape from persecution, enslavement and exploitation.

A solution was offered. "But" Engels remarks, "not in this world."

Another feature of the work is that it is a symbolical representation of contemporary first century politics and John thinks that Jesus' second coming is near at hand. Jesus tells John, "Behold, I come quickly" three times (Revelation 22:7, 12, 20). His failure to show up by now doesn't seem to pose a problem for Christians.

As far as the later Christian religion of love is concerned, Engels reports that you won't find it in Revelation, at least as it regards the enemies of the Christians. There is no cheek turning going on here: it's all fire and brimstone for the foes of Jesus. Engels says, "undiluted revenge is preached." God is even going to completely blot out Rome from the face of the earth. He changed his mind evidently as it is still a popular tourist destination, and the pope has even set up shop there.

As was pointed out earlier the God of John is Yahweh, there is no trinity, it is he, not Christ, who will judge mankind and they will be judged according to their works (no justification by faith here, sorry Luther), no doctrine of original sin, no baptism, and no Eucharist or Mass. Almost every one of these later developments came from Roman and Greek, as well as Egyptian mystery religions. Zoroastrian elements from the Zend–Avesta are also present. These are the ideas that Satan–

the Devil–is an evil force opposed to Yahweh, a great battle between good and evil will occur at the end of time (the final conflict), and that there will be a second coming of Christ. All these ideas were picked up by the Jews during their contact with the Persians before their return after the Babylonian captivity and transmitted to the early Christians.

Once we realize all this, we can also see why Islam was able to rise to the status of a world religion as well. Those areas of the world that were not the homeland of Greco-Roman paganism were open to Islam which spread in areas of Semitic settlement and where Christianity had been imposed by force, so could Islam be.

We will give Engels the last word, the Book of Revelation "shows without any dilution what Judaism, strongly influenced by Alexandria, contributed to Christianity. All that comes later is Western, Greco-Roman addition."

Engels's Dialectics of Nature and the Joy of Cooking

by
Thomas Riggins

One of the chapters (incomplete) in Engels's *Dialectics of Nature* is entitled: "The Part Played by Labour in the Transition from Ape to Man." Although this was written in the 1870s it compares well, I think, with scientific ideas that are considered new today. I propose to compare Engels's views with those reported by Ann Gibbons in an article in the June 15, 2007 issue of *Science* ("Food for Thought: Did the First Cooked Meals Help Fuel the Dramatic Evolutionary Expansion of the Human Brain?").

This article is primarily about Harvard primatologist Richard Wrangham's theory that cooking led to the expansion of the human brain, that is, the *Homo erectus* brain, and resulted in the intellectual development of *Homo sapiens*.

"Wrangham," Gibbons says, "presents cooking as one of the answers to a long-standing riddle in human evolution: Where did humans get the extra energy to support their large brains?" That is, how do we explain that while we use about the same metabolic energy (calorie burning) as apes of comparable size, 25% of our energy is used by our brain, the apes only use 8% for theirs.

Gibbons reports that a classical explanation is that by eating meat we shrank our gastrointestinal system (we need more guts and more time to digest plants than meat) and the saved energy was devoted to the brain. "That theory," she says, "is now gathering additional support."

I don't know why she calls it "classical" because she dates it to 1995. She writes, "Called the expensive tissue hypothesis, this theory was proposed back in 1995..." Here is Engels (who is really "classical") in the 1870s writing about the effects of a meat diet "shortening the time required for digestion." Engels said, "The meat diet, however, had its greatest effect on the brain, which now received a far richer flow of the materials necessary for its nourishment and development, and which, therefore, could develop more rapidly and perfectly from generation to generation." In this respect, modern science has not improved on Engels!

"Wrangham," Gibbons reports, "thinks that in addition, our ancestors got cooking, giving them the same number of calories for less effort." Wrangham first "floated this hypothesis" way back in 1999 (*Science*, 26 March 1999, p. 2004). "There is nothing new under the sun."[19] Here, again, is Engels: "The meat diet led to... the harnessing of fire (which)... still further shortened the digestive process, as it provided the mouth with food already, as it were, half-digested..." Modern science is repeating the views of Engels, and the science of his day, a hundred and thirty years on.

Engels talks about the role of labor in the transition from ape to man, and we shall see that it is labor that is the basis, in humans, for meat eating and cooking. But first, some more of Gibbons.

If cooking led to the expansion of the brain (the modern way of talking about the transition from ape to man), when was the "first supper"? Wrangham thinks it was about 1.6 to 1.9 million years ago (MYA) and the dinner as well as the chef were *Homines erecti*. Of course, Engels knew nothing of modern primate evolution or what a *H. erectus* was, but he did think meat eating and cooking were gradually developed from ape like ancestors (along with speech and more complex thinking), so he would not have been surprised by modern theories.

The article points out that early humans (e.g., australopithecines, 4 to 1.2 MYA) had chimpanzee sized brains, while

H. erectus (AKA *Homo ergaster*) had a brain twice that size (c. 1000 cc[20]). We evolved, along with our cousins the Neandertals, around 500,000 to 200,000 years ago, with brain sizes of about 1300 cc and 1500 cc, respectively. It was meat that allowed the skull to expand for brain growth "according to a long-standing body of evidence." A very long-standing body of evidence since it is found in Engels's article.

We are told the first stone tools, used to butcher animals, date from 2.7 MYA in Ethiopia (at Gona). The cut marks on bones, adjacent fossils, etc., suggest that australopithecines were making these tools and eating meat. Wrangham thinks that *H. erectus* replaced raw meat with cooked meat (1.9 MYA) and this accounts for the big increase in its brain size.

The problem with this theory is that evidence of human use of fire only dates from about 790,000 years ago in what is now Israel. However, this is not fatal to Wrangham's position. Evidence of human controlled fire is very hard to come by and it is quite possible that earlier evidence of fire use will be found.

Some other scientists think Wrangham is right in principle, cooking led to brain increase (as Engels said), but his timeline is off. It didn't happen by *H. erectus*, but by *H. sapiens* and Neanderthals. The jury is out. However, while the jury may be out on Wrangham, it is not out on Engels.

While this article discusses meat and cooking and the theory that "cooking paved the way for brain expansion," it mentions nary a word about the role of labor in expansion of the human brain. The real point of Engels's article should be reaffirmed.

Meat eating and cooking are secondary developments derivative of what Engels called "the decisive step in the transition from ape to man." This was the development of the human hand as a result of the evolution of erect posture in our ancestors. Once the hand was no longer used in locomotion, it was free to develop greater dexterity which "increased from generation to generation"–i.e., was selected for. "Thus," Engels writes, "the hand is not only the organ of labour, it is also the product of labour."

As the first hominids developed more dexterity, they began to make tools and to live under more complex social arrangements, necessitating better communication skills. Thus, Engels writes, "First labour, after it and then with it speech–these were the two most essential stimuli under the influence of which the brain of the ape gradually changed into that of man, which for all its similarity is far larger and more perfect."

I have already mentioned before how Engels saw the adoption of meat eating and fire (cooking) as outgrowths of the labour of primitive humans in tool making (which led to hunting and fishing) which derived from the adoption of upright posture. The australopithecines of Goma represent the earliest tool makers (hominid, that is) and if meat eating led them to develop into *H. erecti*, and Wrangham proves right and *H. erectus* was the first cook, and the *H. erecti*, through the use of fire and cooking, then developed into us, then modern science has validated the argument presented by Engels in his essay of the 1870s.

The prescience of Engels demands that we in the 21st Century continue to profit and learn from his writings. He closes his essay with words that are even more relevant to us today than they were two centuries ago.

After tracing the development of civilization from the time of the transition to modern humans, Engels writes about how our species thinks that it is the master of nature and that we can remake the natural world to our own specifications. But we have to be "reminded that we by no means rule over nature like a conqueror over a foreign people... all our mastery of it consists in the fact that we have the advantage over all other creatures of being able to learn its laws and apply them correctly."

But will we apply them correctly? For that we must rely upon science, and it doesn't look like our political and economic leaders are willing to do that, nor do the masses of people seem properly educated on this necessity.

Engels says that while we have built up a modern civilization (industrial capitalism) by subjecting nature to our immediate interests, we have not calculated the remote long-term effects of our actions. "In relation to nature, as to society, the present mode of production is predominately concerned only about the immediate, the most tangible result..."

As long as the corporations are making their profits, as long as they sell their commodities, they do not care "with what afterwards becomes of the commodity and its purchasers. The same thing applies to the natural effects of the same actions."

So, here we are 130 years down the line with global warming, polluted air, mass extinctions in the plant and animal worlds facing us, and the oceans slowly dying. Engels had hoped that we would by now have had a world socialist community and these problems would not be facing us. But we don't and they are.

There is only one way to solve them, according to Engels, and it "requires something more than mere knowledge. It requires a complete revolution in our hitherto existing mode of production, and simultaneously a revolution in our whole contemporary social order." We had better get to work. Time is running out!

Notes

[1] A 1973 Sydney Pollack film.

[2] Preface to *The Philosophy of Right*.

[3] Book by Marx and Engels published in 1845.

[4] Joe Sims, *Ten Best and Worst Ideas of Marxism,* 2008.

[5] This quote is attributed to Arnold Toynbee.

[6] The term Pygmies Engels is using here is not referring to the African tribe, but to the old, etymological use of the word as a synonym to short.

[7] Among savages and lower barbarians the idea is still universal that the human forms which appear in dreams are souls which have temporarily left their bodies; the real man is, therefore, held responsible for acts committed by his dream apparition against the dreamer. Thus author Everard im Thurn found this belief current, for example, among the Indians of Guiana in 1884.

[8] The countries of the West, especially Europe and America. Contrasted with orient.

[9] Unknown or unexplored territory.

[10] The schoolmaster of Sadowa: An expression currently at the time by German bourgeois publicists after the victory of the Prussians at Sadowa (in the Austro-Prussian War of 1866), the implications being that the Prussian victory was to be attributed to the superiority of the Prussian system of public education.

[11] The son of Zeus and Europa, and brother of Minos, who, as a ruler and judge in the underworld, was renowned for his justice.

[12] Here I may be permitted to make a personal explanation. Lately, repeated reference has been made to my share in this theory, and so I can hardly avoid saying a few words here to settle this point. I cannot deny that both before and during my 40 year collaboration with Marx I had a certain independent share in laying the foundation of the theory, and more particularly in its elaboration. But the greater part of its leading basic principles, especially in the realm of economics and history, and, above all, their final trenchant formulation, belong to Marx. What I contributed–at any rate with the exception of my work in a few special fields–Marx could very well have done without me. What Marx accomplished I would not have achieved. Marx stood higher, saw further, and took a wider and quicker view than all the rest of us. Marx was a genius; we others were at best talented. Without him the theory would not be by far what it is today. If therefore rightly bears his name.

[13] See *Das Wesen der menschlichen Kopfarbeit, dargestellt von einem Handarbeiter* (The Nature of Human Brainwork, Described by a Manual Worker) Hamburg, Meissner.

[14] Roman historian.

[15] A citizen of a town or city, typically a member of the wealthy bourgeoisie.

[16] The members of a heretical sect in southern France in the 12th–13th centuries, identified with the Cathars. Their teaching was a form of Manichaean dualism, with an extremely strict moral and social code.

[17] This article was written for the 200th anniversary of Engels birth in 2020.

[18] This article was originally published on Christmas day 2020 and references Engels's article "On the History of Early Christianity" originally published in *Die Neue Zeit* and is referenced throughout all three parts of this essay.

[19] Ecclesiastes 1:9

[20] This is in reference to cranial capacity.